TURN IT AROUND

TURN IT AROUND

A Different Direction for a New Life

FRANK SANTORA

HOWARD BOOKS
A DIVISION OF SIMON & SCHUSTER, INC.
New York · Nashville · London · Toronto · Sydney

Published by Howard Books, a division of Simon & Schuster, Inc.
1230 Avenue of the Americas, New York, NY 10020

Turn It Around: A Different Direction for a New Life © 2010 Frank Santora

Library of Congress Cataloging-in-Publication Data
Santora, Frank.
Turn it around: a different direction for a new life / Frank Santora.
p. cm.
Includes bibliographical references
1. Christian life. 2. Suffering—Religious aspects—Christianity. 3. Failure (Psychology)—Religious aspects—Christianity. 4. Consolation. I. Title.
BV4909.S26 2010
248.8'6—dc22   2009039155
978-1-4165-9757-5
978-1-4391-7088-5 (ebook)

10 9 8 7 6 5 4 3 2 1

HOWARD colophon is a registered trademark of Simon & Schuster, Inc.

Manufactured in the United States of America

For information regarding special discounts for bulk purchases, please contact: Simon & Schuster Special Sales at 1-800-456-6798 or business@simonandschuster.com.

The Simon & Schuster Speakers Bureau can bring authors to your live event. For more information or to book an event, contact the Simon & Schuster Speakers Bureau at 1-866-248-3049 or visit our website at www.simonspeakers.com.

Edited by Between the Lines

Cover design by ThinkPen Design

Interior design by Fritz Metsch

For my wife, Lisa,

and our children, Nicole and Joseph,

whose unconditional love, trust, support, and inspiration

continually reinforce my belief in a God

who can turn our lives around

no matter what trials we face.

CONTENTS

FOREWORD

Success in life is more than just a reward for wishful thinking. It also requires inspiration, commitment, and action. Even for those of us in command of all those qualities, though, moving forward toward the achievement of a goal can be challenging—especially at a time like ours, when traditional values that promote stability are being questioned, ignored, or even attacked.

In just the past few months, I've spoken as a religious counselor with individuals confronting and questioning their sexuality, with others who have lost their jobs and even their homes, and with still others who are suffering from life-threatening physical ailments without the benefit of health insurance to help them with the astronomical and ever-rising medical expenses. All that, plus the recent near-record-breaking drop in stock values and a devastating series of natural disasters, is, lamentably, even causing many people to question their faith. A young man I spoke with recently who, although just twenty-three years old, has gone through the pain and emotional distress of two heart-transplant operations, told me he has come to wonder whether God really exists—adding that if he does exist, it would seem that he doesn't really care about us.

We need to remember, of course, that God never promised us life would be easy. But he did make another kind of promise. As the apostle Paul told believers in Corinth, "God is faithful, who will not allow you to be tempted beyond what you are able, but with the temptation will also make the way of escape, that you may be able to bear it" (1 Corinthians 10:13 NKJV).

On that occasion Paul was specifically teaching about the ability and willingness of God to turn our lives around when we're in the grip of temptation, but the implication of God's promise goes beyond the particular to include trials and tribulations of all kinds. So those of us who are in trouble because we've made bad choices along the way, for instance, need not surrender to the fear that there is no way out for us. God is our ally, and he can turn our lives around!

My friend Frank Santora's book *Turn It Around* is more than just a good read. In fact, it could well be the key to the breakthrough you've been seeking. As you read it, you will be reminded that, unlike our troubled economy, God is not in recession, nor is he, like many of us, nervous and bewildered. He has a personalized plan of action for each of us and can turn our lives around!

Alvin Slaughter
Worship leader, author, speaker
Alvin Slaughter International

TURN IT AROUND

1

LOOKING FOR THE
GOOD IN LIFE

✣

HAS LIFE EVER HANDED you a double whammy? In 2007 life clob-
bered me with a classic one-two punch, hitting me with a blow to
my church ministry for starters and then following with a jab to
my personal finances. It all started when the school the church operates saw it's budget reduced by $350,000. When you have teach-
ers' salaries to pay, that's not a loss you can shrug off. The second
blow came when a bank loan my wife and I were relying on for a
business venture fell through. Based on the bank's commitment
letter, we had signed a land lease and hired contractors. Then the
bank dropped out right before closing, and suddenly we had a several thousand dollar monthly lease, contractors wanting payment,
and no loan to cover any of it.

I didn't know where our church was going to get the money to
keep the school going. And I didn't know where I was going to get
the money to keep our business going.

I began having sleepless nights. Often I would lie awake, with
either the church needs or our family finances, or both, running
through my mind. In the middle of the night I would get up and
grab my journal and write prayers to God, feebly pleading for help.
Then I would wait for God to give me wisdom. I'd sit for three or
four hours, waiting for God to do something, to answer me, to give

me something—anything—but nothing would come. I wouldn't feel any better; I would feel worse. Soon I was thinking, *Why do I even bother praying? I feel worse now!* Or, *Why isn't God giving me an answer to any of this?* This went on night after night.

I suspect you've had times in your life like that. Maybe you're going through that time right now—not in the details, of course, but sometimes it's not the details that matter; it's what you're feeling.

- Feeling that you're headed down the wrong road
- Feeling that you've blown it
- Feeling that no one believes in you
- Feeling that you've walked away from God and can't ever get back
- Feeling that things are out of your control
- Feeling that you're trapped and have nowhere to go
- Feeling that in a world of billions of people, there couldn't possibly be anything special about you

It doesn't matter if you feel all of these things or just one. You desperately want a way to turn life around.

I felt that desperation in 2007. My sleepless nights had me questioning everything, from the real to the absurd. I was trapped in what Max Lucado calls the "Whaddiffs and Howells."[1] What if I had waited to sign that lease? How will we keep the school open? What if what I'm hoping for doesn't happen? How will we pay for our children's education? My mind was in turmoil, and my body and soul joined in.

One morning, after another sleepless night, I spent some time—as I do every morning—with God. At first I just shared my hurt with him as I always did, telling him how overwhelmed I was and how hopeless things seemed to me—as if he didn't already know that. All of a sudden, in the midst of my pitiful complaints, the Holy Spirit took over. Instead of sharing my hurts with God, I began to share my heart with him. I went from telling God how overwhelmed I was to saying how much I loved him and needed him.

That's when God spoke directly to my heart. And this is what he said: *"Don't worry. I work all things together for the good for those who love me and are called according to my purpose."*

That promise is also found in Romans 8:28. Now, I realize there's probably a strict theological meaning to that verse, but sometimes we can destroy a verse of Scripture by getting so theological with it that we miss what God is saying to us directly in our moment of need. So when God said that to me, I simply heard, *"Don't worry, my son. I will turn it around."* And then, because pastors can be just as hardheaded as the next guy, God took everything I'd been thinking . . . and answered. Into all my feelings of doubt and despair, God inserted his promises:

- I will turn your life around when you're on the wrong road.
- I will turn your life around when you've blown it.
- I will turn your life around when no one believes in you.
- I will turn your life around when you've walked away from me.
- I will turn your life around when things are out of your control.
- I will turn your life around when you're trapped and have nowhere to go.
- I will turn your life around because you're special to me.

Those words may not sound like much to you now, but they meant everything to me when I needed help. I immediately stopped what I was doing and ran to my nightstand drawer, pulled out a notepad and the stubbiest little pencil you ever saw, and began to write down God's promises. At first I was writing just for myself; but then I realized that God wasn't speaking only to me. He sends that same message to all of us. Every moment of our lives, God offers these promises to us. He reminds us of these promises again and again through our own lives and the lives of others. We just have to stop and notice.

That's the first step—realizing that God can be doing good things for us in the midst of all that is happening to us, even when we can't see any good. We must look for and focus on those good things. If we don't—if we persist in focusing only on the negative things that are troubling us—we'll be trapped in the very rut from which we want to escape.

Let's look at that verse that God spoke to my heart: "We know that in all things God works for the good of those who love him, who have been called according to his purpose" (Romans 8:28).

Notice that God didn't say he causes bad things; neither did he say that everything that happens is good. But he did say that, for those who love him, he *will bring good* out of all the bad things that happen. That verse tells us—promises us—that even in the midst of bad, God is causing good to take place. Even though we think our lives are falling apart, we need to look for the good. It may feel to us like we're in a whirlwind, but if we trust in God, if we look with the eyes of faith, we'll see in the end that God was at work. Even though God isn't pulling the strings on the bad events, his divine hand of providence is on everything; he is causing those stressful, painful, horrible circumstances to turn around for our good. When we look for the good, we find so many incredible things that we never would have seen if we hadn't looked for them in the midst of our troubles.

Looking for good isn't usually our first inclination when we experience trouble. It's not always easy, but we can get better at it with a little awareness and practice. One way we can learn to look for the good God is doing in our lives is by observing the good God has accomplished in others through their difficulties. Numerous stories tell of good emerging from the midst of troubling or even disastrous circumstances. For example, in 1883 a devastating tornado tore through Rochester, Minnesota, killing and injuring many in the small city. A local surgeon named William Worrall Mayo and his two sons—also skilled physicians—labored day and night to care for the tornado victims. They asked for no reward, responding only out of concern for others. Moved by their efforts, Mother Alfred Moes of the local Sisters of Saint Francis approached Dr. Mayo and his sons about establishing a hospital. When the three physicians agreed, Mother Alfred and her fellow nuns raised the money for a state-of-the-art facility, which opened in 1889. From the midst of tragedy came events that led to the founding of the Mayo Clinic, one of the most celebrated medical treatment and research centers in the world.[2]

God doesn't cause tragedy, but he excels at turning it around for good—and God's good is bigger than anything we can imagine. If he can bring healing for millions out of the devastation of a tornado, he can certainly bring about good from our smaller struggles.

We don't have to look far to discover how God can take personal tragedies and turn them around. For example, I can't think of a more painful and faith-challenging trial than the loss of physical senses. We relate to the world through sight and sound in order to live our everyday lives. What would your life be like if you lost one of the senses you rely on most? Now try to imagine what a brilliant and dedicated musician would suffer should he lose his hearing. Surely the ability to hear would be essential to a musician's success. At the age of thirty-one, Ludwig van Beethoven began to go deaf.[3] He had developed a reputation as a skilled composer and performer, yet he had accomplished so little of what he felt capable. As his condition worsened, depression overwhelmed him. "O how harshly was I pushed back by the double sad experience of my bad hearing," he wrote of his loss. "A little more and I would have ended my life."[4]

Any one of us might understand these feelings—we, too, might be tempted to give up after such a blow to our life plans. But Beethoven refused to give in. Though he could no longer hear the notes, he continued to write music. He composed many of his greatest works, including his masterpiece, the Ninth Symphony—and its majestic "Ode to Joy"—after becoming completely deaf. God brought good to Beethoven even in his tragedy, filling his imagination with sounds and rhythms even more glorious than those he had once actually been able to hear.

God made good triumph over misfortune for another musician, Fanny Crosby, composer of many of America's most beloved hymns. As an infant, Fanny was deprived of one of the senses that most of us deem essential to daily living: sight. Fanny's potentially tragic story began when she developed an eye infection only weeks after her birth. In the absence of her regular physician, her parents foolishly consulted a man claiming to be a doctor who insisted on treating the condition with hot poultices.

Fanny's mother, Mercy, was horrified by the child's screams, which increased in volume and became more and more anguished as the "doctor" persisted in his treatment. She protested that her baby was so tiny and in such obvious pain that perhaps they ought to wait for their regular doctor to return. But the charlatan prevailed, insisting that putting off treatment could lead to terrible consequences, and Fanny's distressed mother reluctantly accepted the treatment.

Fanny's screams eventually diminished to a pitiful whimper, but they lingered in Mercy's memory. The infection in Fanny's eyes went away on its own, but her corneas had been burned by the bogus treatment, and white scars began to form over her eyes. In the weeks that followed, John and Mercy Crosby realized that Fanny was not responding to visual stimuli. Their worst fears were confirmed when they learned that little Fanny was now totally blind.

When the tragedy became known, the practitioner fled in fear for his life. Fanny never recovered her sight, and to add to the family's misery, her father died of illness that same year.[5]

Despite everything, young Fanny, with the help of her mother and grandmother, maintained a positive attitude, never allowing her blindness to diminish her faith in God and his ability to do great things through her. Fanny prevailed over her disability and used her phonographic memory to her advantage, learning several books of the Bible by heart. In adulthood she became one of the nation's most celebrated popular poets and hymn writers, penning more than nine thousand hymns and poems, perhaps the best known of which is "Blessed Assurance"—Fanny's personal testimony to the world.

But in view of her lifelong blindness, the message of her hymn "My Savior First of All" and a subsequent comment she made are especially touching and inspiring.

> *When my lifework is ended, and I cross the swelling tide,*
> *When the bright and glorious morning I shall see;*
> *I shall know my Redeemer when I reach the other side,*
> *And His smile will be the first to welcome me.*
>
> *I shall know Him, I shall know Him,*
> *And redeemed by His side I shall stand,*
> *I shall know Him, I shall know Him,*
> *By the print of the nails in His hand.*
>
> *Oh, the soul-thrilling rapture when I view His blessed face,*
> *And the luster of His kindly beaming eye;*
> *How my full heart will praise Him for the mercy, love and grace,*
> *That prepare for me a mansion in the sky.*

A pastor once sympathetically said to Fanny, "I think it is a great pity that the Master did not give you sight when he showered so many other gifts upon you." Fanny quickly replied, "Do you know that if at birth I had been able to make one petition, it would have been that I was born blind?" Stunned by her response, the minister asked her why she would wish such a thing. Fanny replied, "Because, when I get to heaven, the first face that shall ever gladden my sight will be that of my Savior!"[6]

Fanny often spoke of being blind as a blessing. She credited her blindness for opening a door into education, gaining her admission to the New York Institute for the Blind—an opportunity her poor family otherwise could not have afforded. She said blindness left her free to concentrate, led her to develop her remarkable memory, and helped her create an emotional connection with audiences that made her widely acclaimed as a speaker. Indeed, every good thing Fanny experienced in life she would directly link to her "tragic" loss of sight—so much so that she once said she didn't blame the doctor at all—in fact, she said, "He unwittingly did me the greatest favor in the world."[7]

Fanny's songs and poetry ultimately brought her before Congress and at least eight presidents. God took all the things that happened in Fanny's life and wove them together into something wondrously good.

One more story.

Perhaps you've heard of Vice Admiral James Stockdale, who was captured during the Vietnam War and frequently tortured during his seven-year imprisonment. Although he was not given the rights due him as a prisoner under the Geneva Conventions—no set release date or even any assurance that he would survive to see his family again—he shouldered the burden of command, doing everything he could to create conditions that would increase the number of prisoners who would survive with their spirits and honor unbroken. At one point, then Commander Stockdale learned that as the highest-ranking prisoner, he would be paraded in front of a group of foreign journalists and used as a propaganda tool. Knowing that his captors were not treating his men well, as they claimed, but were torturing and mistreating them, Stockdale beat himself with a stool and cut his scalp with a razor, deliberately disfiguring himself so his captors could not show him off as an example of a "well-treated prisoner." When told that some of his men had died under torture, Stockdale slashed his own wrists, declaring that he would die rather than assist his captors. Afraid of the backlash if the highest-ranking officer died under their care, and convinced Stockdale would die before he'd cooperate with them, the Vietnamese abandoned their attempts at coercion through torture. Stockdale's refusal to give in—and that same attitude he inspired in his fellow prisoners—eventually led to better treatment for the POWs as the war drew to a close.[8]

Stockdale survived the cruelty of the "Hanoi Hilton" and returned home to eventually rise to the rank of Vice Admiral. "I never lost faith in the end of the story," Stockdale said, reflecting on his experiences. "I never doubted not only that I would get out, but also that I would prevail in the end and turn the experience into the defining event of my life, which, in retrospect, I would not trade."[9] He never lost faith in a positive outcome—faith in the end of the story!

That surely must remind you of the scripture we've been considering. Let's take it from a different translation this time: "We know that God causes everything to work together for the good of those who love God and are called according to his purpose for them" (Romans 8:28 NLT). And what does that mean? It means that we must never lose faith in the end of the story. Remember that it's God who is writing your story. No matter how many bad things may come up in the course of your life, if you do your part by keeping faith and focusing on the good, God will work everything together for good and surprise and amaze you with a happy ending.

So come along with me in the pages that follow to see how God can turn your life around . . .

   . . . when you're on the wrong road.

   . . . when you've blown it.

. . . when no one believes in you.

. . . when you've walked away from him.

. . . when things seem out of your control.

. . . when you feel trapped and seemingly have nowhere to go.

God wants to help you . . . because you're special to him!

2

TURNING AROUND
WHEN YOU'RE ON THE
WRONG ROAD

We were late. My wife and I were on our way to a surprise party being given for one of our close friends. Neither of us had ever been to the house before, but I was driving, and I was sure I'd have no trouble finding it.

As often happens to me, though, I took a wrong turn—and then another—until I was hopelessly lost.

I'm terrible at directions. So bad, in fact, that without help I can almost never retrace my steps to find where I got off course and get back on the right road. And so God has taken pity on me and given me a wife who seems to have a built-in GPS. That's a real blessing when we travel, because—both on the road and in life—the direction we take determines where we end up.

Surprisingly, though we understand the importance of direction when we're driving, biking, skateboarding, jogging, or whatever, too often we fail to take it into account when we're setting and pursuing a goal in life.

Andy Stanley, pastor of Atlanta's North Point Community Church, explains the importance of direction in life this way. He says most of us come up with an impressive list of great intentions for our lives, but we don't follow up with our actions. For example:

- We want to retire early and live in luxury, but we don't start saving until we're fifty.
- We want top-tier professional careers, but we don't pursue education to gain the skills.
- We want a close-knit family, but we spend all our time at our jobs.
- We want our children to respect us, but we disappoint them with our behavior.
- We want to grow old and enjoy our grandchildren, but we ignore our health.
- We want to lose weight, but we indulge our appetites.
- We want a deep, loving connection with our spouses, but we put the children first.
- We want to know God intimately, but every morning we read the news instead of the Bible.

Then when we don't get the things we want in spite of all our good intentions, we become disappointed, frustrated with life, envious of others, and angry with God. We forget that "the road to hell is paved with good intentions" and ignore what Andy Stanley calls the Path Principle: "Direction, not good intentions, determines destination."[1]

Finding Direction

We tend to be better at judging wrong paths in others than in ourselves. People tell us stories about how they've ended up where they are now, and before they're halfway through their tales of woe, we can see where and why they went wrong. We often can see where the paths others are on are going to take them, yet we tend to be blind to where our own paths are taking us. Whether we're just clueless or we're lying to ourselves, we start down the same wrong paths we know others shouldn't take, convinced that in our case it'll be okay.

But it won't be, because direction determines destination. When you go down the wrong path, the path eventually becomes a highway. And when you're on a highway going in the wrong direction, you're not going to reach your desired destination—you're just losing time. Now, time might be all you lose when you're driving, but when you're on the highway of life, the loss can be much greater. Going in the wrong direction could cost you your spouse, your children, your job, your peace, your reputation, your sanity, or even your security. Much is at stake when we head down the wrong path in life!

That's why we should rejoice in the knowledge that, when we're headed in the wrong direction, God can turn our lives around.

Andy Stanley's Path Principle tells us that it's not our intentions but the direction we *choose* that determines our destination in life. And what we choose depends on what catches our attention—or what we choose to give our attention to. Simply choosing to give our attention to the wrong thing can lead to dangerous consequences. We all know that when we're driving, we need to keep our eyes straight ahead—on the road. If we choose to look either to the right or the left, we might veer off in that direction or fail to see a danger in the road in front of us. Either possibility might lead to an accident.

Sometimes what catches our attention can lead to a more positive result. When I was eighteen years old, a beautiful young woman named Lisa caught my attention. (I must have grabbed her attention, too, because she became my wife.) The moment she caught my attention, I stopped following my original path and plan and switched to another—a better one. My path—and subsequently my life—was forever changed. When Lisa's father relocated to Connecticut, Lisa and I decided to move there too. We soon became so warmly and enthusiastically involved in our new church that I quit my old job as an accountant and accepted a position as the church's assistant pastor, though at an enormous decrease in salary. I had no idea then that my new path would lead me to a destination where I would find myself the head pastor of one of the largest churches in the state.

So the greatest determining influence for the path we take in life and the destination to which it will lead is either what grabs our attention or that on which we choose to focus our attention. Mercifully, even when we're focused on the wrong things, hurtling toward destruction on the wrong path, God often stops us and forces us to turn our attention to him so that he can start to turn our lives around.

Road Signs from God

In the movie *Bruce Almighty*, the main character, played by Jim Carrey, is driving down the road, mad at the world and mad at God, and he cries out, "God, please give me a sign!" Just then a truck filled with Danger signs passes right in front of him.

That's a joke, of course, but the truth is, God loves to send us road signs—those surreal moments when we're praying, asking God to show up, and in that moment the unexpected happens—the phone rings, and a friend says, "Hey, you're on my heart, and I just felt like I really needed to give you a call." Or we're reading the Bible and the passage speaks perfectly to the question on our hearts.

I've encountered my own road signs from God, and I've had the joy of unknowingly offering God's road signs to others. Many times people will come up to me after a church service and say, "Pastor, I can't believe you spoke about that topic today. I was asking God specifically about this, and then you talked about it! It felt like God's answer just for me." One significant example of this happened not long ago. I was delivering a sermon and was overcome by a feeling that someone in the service had prayed, *"God, if you're real and want to help me, then please ask the pastor to call me up at the end of the service to pray for me."* So I did just that. As I closed the service, I said, "I know this doesn't have anything to do with what I spoke about today, but I feel as if somebody here, right before church this morning, said to God: 'If you're real, have the pastor call me up.' If that person is you, I want to pray with you." Immediately a young woman rose from her seat and came to the front with tears in her eyes. God had given her a road sign that turned her around and settled her question.

The Bible gives us another illustration of someone who was headed down the wrong path when God put up road signs to turn him in the right direction. That person was a man named Saul, who later became known as the apostle Paul. And the wrong path he was on was a literal road—the road to Damascus.

When we first meet Saul, he's a powerful religious enthusiast with considerable influence among the Sanhedrin, the ruling religious authority in Jerusalem. Saul was vehemently opposed to any and all followers of "the Way" (believers in Jesus as the Messiah), and he was especially incensed at the suggestion that Jesus had risen from the dead. Saul's main objective in life seemed to be to kill or imprison these believers. Indeed, the first time we meet him in Scripture, he's encouraging the stoning of one of Jesus' most faithful followers, Stephen, who had provoked the wrath of the religious leaders by declaring Christ as God. You can easily picture this impassioned young man cheering the mob on, admonishing the stone throwers to use even bigger rocks as Stephen bled to death under their blows. Saul was about as opposed to Jesus and the gospel as one can get, seeming a more likely candidate for God's wrath than God's kindness.

After Stephen's death, a general persecution of Jesus' followers broke out. Most believers in Jerusalem fled for their lives, many to Damascus, Syria, roughly 150 miles northeast of Jerusalem. Saul pursued them, vowing to capture, imprison, or kill those who had fled. Damascus was a strategic commercial area where many trade routes met, and Saul may have been afraid that if the message about Jesus took hold there, it might spread through the whole Roman Empire. He was determined not to let that happen on his watch. So he headed down the Damascus Road—for him, the wrong road— looking for blood.

This is what happened:

> Saul was still breathing out murderous threats against the Lord's disciples. He went to the high priest and asked him for letters to the synagogues in Damascus, so that if he found any there who be- longed to the Way, whether men or women, he might take them as prisoners to Jerusalem. As he neared Damascus on his journey, sud- denly a light from heaven flashed around him. He fell to the ground and heard a voice say to him, "Saul, Saul, why do you persecute me?"
>
> "Who are you, Lord?" Saul asked.
>
> "I am Jesus, whom you are persecuting," he replied.[2]

Now that's a road sign even Saul couldn't miss.

When we're on the wrong road, God often uses a series of road signs to turn us around and get us back on the path where we be- long. Saul's Damascus Road experience illustrates such road signs and serves as an example for us when God is helping us to turn it around. What are these signs? Let's take a look.

ROAD SIGN #1: STOP!

Stop! That's the road sign God slapped in front of Saul as he traveled down the wrong road. And Saul stopped.

A simple course correction—veering a little this way or that— might work when we're just slightly off track. But when we're speeding blindly the wrong way down the road, drastic action is needed. When you're on the highway and suspect you might be going in the wrong direction, what do you do? If you're smart, you'll pull over and stop so you can reassess—figure out where you are and decide how to get back to where you should be.

But when we're oblivious to the error of our ways? That's when it helps to have someone with built-in, unerring GPS who loves us and wants what's best for us. God knows when we're off track, and he knows when we're hurtling down a road toward spiritual or physical danger. *"Stop!"* God says. *"Don't go any farther down the wrong road."* When God flashes a stop sign in our path, we can be sure it's not because he's some cosmic killjoy who wants to keep us from reaching the destination we desire. Rather, he's intent on helping us reach our divinely intended destiny. He stops us in our tracks, gets our attention, and challenges our assumptions.

Look back at the story of Saul. Did you notice how the whole event caught him so by surprise that all he could do was stammer out the question, "Who are you?" And the answer that came like a lightning bolt was a life-changing revelation: "I am Jesus."

That answer stopped Saul—his mission, his core beliefs, his life's work. It instantly changed everything. Remember that Saul was dead set against considering the idea that Jesus, who had been crucified, had also been resurrected from the dead. So try to imagine the impact the voice of this Jesus must have had on him. In an instant Saul realized he had been wrong. He'd been heading down the wrong road. He was guilty of consenting to and encouraging the stoning of a man, Stephen, whom Saul now knew had been innocent of blasphemy when he proclaimed Jesus as Lord. Imagine how Saul must have felt—exposed, ashamed, and confused. He had no idea what to say or do. But he could no longer continue down his old road.

Sometimes God stops us and grabs our attention in spectacular ways. For Saul it was a voice from heaven. Most of us won't have the same kind of experience he had, because God works according to our individual needs and circumstances. But God will give signs to those who are willing to see. He will speak to those willing to listen. Why? Because that's his nature. He cares about each of us. He wants only the best for us. It breaks his heart to see us continually fouling up our lives, so he tries to make himself known. Over a lifetime he speaks again and again. If we listen, we will hear him.

However he does it, God is so committed to turning our lives around and setting us in the direction of the divine destiny he intends for us that he will stop us from continuing down the wrong road even if our lives may seem to be lost causes!

God believes in rescuing "lost causes." When Saul was lying on the ground, he didn't know what to expect. Was it payback time for all he'd done?

But Jesus didn't punish him; he simply said it was time to turn around. Jesus told Saul, "Get up and go into the city, and you will be told what you must do."[3]

The book of Acts also tells us, "The men traveling with Saul stood there speechless; they heard the sound but did not see anyone. Saul got up from the ground, but when he opened his eyes he could see nothing. So they led him by the hand into Damascus. For three days he was blind, and did not eat or drink anything."[4]

Later in his life, when Paul recounts this story, he adds that the men who were with him saw the light but did not understand what the voice said.[5] Why didn't God permit anyone else to understand what Saul heard? I believe it was because God wanted to transform Saul, not embarrass him. I believe that being headed down the wrong road is a personal thing between God and us and that God wants to keep it that way.

ROAD SIGN #2: YIELD

Did you notice the second road sign God put in Saul's path? It was "Yield." Once God had stopped Saul from continuing down the wrong road, the next important step was for Saul to yield himself and his will to God's. That's how he would find his way onto the right road. But how would God get the stiff-necked and independent Saul to yield?

Pain is often the vehicle God uses to teach his children to yield. It's what he used with Saul.

When Saul got up, he found that he was blind. Imagine the terror and psychological pain of being without sight—especially in an unfamiliar place. Would you ever see again? How would you know where to go and how to get there? How could you be safe if you couldn't even see a pothole in the road, much less a person who wanted to harm you? We don't know if Saul's blind eyes hurt physically, but it's not hard to imagine the emotional pain he felt.

Pain like this may seem a strange tool for God to use to help turn a life around, but sometimes that's exactly what it takes. Pain has a way of getting our attention, altering our behavior, and getting us to change. We change because we want to get rid of the pain, whether it's physical or emotional, whether it's caused by a wound or by negative opinions others have of us. Pain knocks us off balance and helps us realize that we can't fix everything ourselves. We need someone else: God.

Because change is difficult, we generally try to resist it. As Isaac Newton observed in his first law of motion, "Every body continues in its state of rest, or of uniform motion in a right line, unless it is compelled to change that state by forces impressed upon it."[6] That law can be applied to you and me: we tend to stay the way we are or continue going the way we're going unless we are compelled to change by some force impressed upon us—a force such as pain. Only then do some people yield to God.

It was imperative for Saul to yield to God's will, for God wasn't just building an average citizen, content to live out his life without leaving any lasting mark on the world. God's purpose was to fashion from the yielded Saul a warrior for his kingdom; an apostle of apostles; a writer of much of the New Testament; a cornerstone of the church; a man who would go from waging war on the church to waging war against hell; a first-century Rambo who would be beaten with rods but keep going, shipwrecked but keep going, stoned but keep going, thrown into prison but keep going, left for dead but keep going. He was transforming Saul into Paul, and God chose pain as his transformational tool that would help Saul yield to God's plan and power.

Pain forces us to rely on God. We know that we must break an animal's independent spirit before we can lead it, train it, or work with it. For horses, the procedure is called breaking the horse. Other animals—eagles, for instance—must also be broken before they can be trained and led.

In the remote mountainous regions of Kazakhstan and Kyrgyzstan live men who train eagles for hunting, a centuries-old practice. The method for training these majestic birds, however cruel it may seem, is so ancient it has become ritual, a tradition passed from father to son. Captured when newly hatched or barely out of the nest, a young bird is immediately blinded with a hood. Unable to see, it's kept in a cage designed to rock without ceasing. Disoriented and constantly having to maintain its balance, the young bird is unable to sleep. The hunter does not feed the bird for up to three days, only chanting and singing to it endlessly, so that the bird tunes its hearing to the master's voice. After three days, the hunter strokes the bird, feeding it by hand, continuing to talk to it. Soon the relationship between eagle and hunter becomes unbreakable, the bird relying solely on its new master for everything. The bird's loyalty is fierce and lifelong—the hunter doesn't even need a leash or hood. The eagle will always return to its master.[7]

The principle is a simple one. For God to be able to lead us down the right path, we often must first have our rebellious, self-centered spirits broken. Until we come to a place where we will allow ourselves to be led, God will not lead us. We can find illustrations throughout the Bible that tell of how pain broke people of their independent spirits so they might yield to God and rely on him alone.

Perhaps you've heard of Jabez. He's one in a long, tortuous recitation of names you'll find in the genealogy recorded in 1 Chronicles 4: Jabez stands out from the other names in the list because he's the only one with a story. The writer pauses to comment, "Jabez was more honorable than his brothers, and his mother called his name Jabez, saying, 'Because I bore him in pain.' "[8] The brief interlude almost shouts at us, as if to say, *"Pay attention to this: it's important!"* It's as though the writer of the book of 1 Chronicles was being moved by God to give us a message, to point out the instrument God uses to cause us to yield to him so he can turn around our off-track lives.

Names are important in the Bible. Throughout the Scriptures, a child's name is a commentary on his character or the plight of the parents at the time of the birth. For instance:

- The name *Isaac* means "laughter." It was chosen because Isaac's mother laughed when told she would bear a child in her old age.
- *Jacob* means "supplanter" or "one who is cunning or clever or who tricks." True to his name, Jacob tricked his brother out of his birthright.
- Naomi named her sons *Mahlon* and *Kilion*, which mean "Puny" and "Pining": both of them died in early adulthood.
- *Solomon* means "peace," and he was the first king of Israel who did not go to war.
- *Jesus* means "God saves," and *Emmanuel* means "God is with us."

God likes to make a point with names.

You've got to admit there's something strange about a mother who names her son Jabez because she bore him in pain. What could

she have been thinking? Maybe that birth was an especially difficult one. Perhaps she was in labor for an unusually long time.

But can you imagine what it was like for Jabez growing up? Every mention of his name would have been a reminder that he was a
causer of pain. "Oh, no, here comes Pain." "We don't want Pain on
our team." "You really are a Pain, you know."

Jabez's name put him in a box and influenced what everyone
thought of and expected from him. And when you grow up in an
environment where everyone thinks of you in a certain way, after
a while it's easy to start believing it yourself.

Yet the pain so intertwined with Jabez's beginning and his fate
forced him to rely on God to turn his life around. We know this
because the second of the two verses devoted to Jabez tells us,
"Jabez called on the God of Israel saying, 'Oh, that You would bless
me indeed, and enlarge my territory, that Your hand would be with
me, and that You would keep me from evil, that I may not cause
pain!' So God granted him what he requested."[9]

Jabez was smart enough to realize that what he could not do for
himself, God could do for him. Yes, we can yield to God and turn
to him for help without the catalyst of pain. But often pain is the
spur that pushes us to yield our wills to God and cry out to him for
help to turn our lives around for the better.

Through pain we find God's strength. He tells us: "My power is
made perfect in weakness."[10] Years down the road, the apostle Paul
had learned to actually rejoice in his own weaknesses, proclaiming
that because of God, "When I am weak, then I am strong!"[11] That
giant of the faith discovered God's strength through the pain he
experienced, beginning that fateful day on the road to Damascus.
Perhaps pain isn't as bad a thing as we think.

Dr. Paul W. Brand was well known for his expertise treating
leprosy as the head of the leprosarium in Carville, Louisiana. Until
his death he was in demand the world over for his insightful lec-
tures on the subject. But one trip to London turned frightening.

The ocean voyage had been exhausting, followed immediately by an uncomfortable train ride from the port. As Dr. Brand prepared for bed, he removed his shoes, pulled off a sock, and noticed he had no nerve sensation in his heel. Most of us would have thought nothing of it—just a little numbness. But Dr. Brand knew that nerve damage is a key symptom of leprosy. Although he had lectured for years that leprosy imposed no risk of infection beyond a certain stage, the loss of feeling in his heel terrified him. What if he'd been wrong? Then, not only Dr. Brand, but all his staff—anyone who treated leprosy—might become infected by a disease with no cure.

Alarmed but determined to know the truth, Dr. Brand jabbed his foot with a pin, pushing far enough to draw a drop of blood. He felt no pain; his nerves were deadened.

He lay awake throughout the night, fearing that his life as a surgeon was over. He would become a patient, forced to leave his family. He would have to warn his staff that he had been wrong—that all of them were in danger of contracting the hideous disease.

When morning came, Dr. Brand decided to try again. Once again he took the pin, centered it over the same spot he had pricked before, and stabbed. The sudden sting caused him to shout in pain.

Dorothy Clarke Wilson describes Brand's reaction in the biography *Ten Fingers for God*: "What an absolutely glorious sensation . . . to feel that sharp painful thrust of the pin!"[12] Dr. Brand realized that during the long train ride, sitting immobile, he had numbed a nerve. He didn't have leprosy at all. From then on, as Wilson says, whenever Dr. Brand experienced pain from "cutting a finger, turning an ankle . . . even suffering from agonizing nausea as his body reacted in violent self-protection from mushroom poisoning, he was to respond in fervent gratitude, 'Thank God for pain!' "[13]

Yes, indeed, thank God for pain. Pain wakes us up. Pain makes us look heavenward. Pain makes us ready to listen—ready to yield to God. We're all like the little boy who reached into the cookie jar when Mom wasn't looking and shoveled too many cookies into his mouth. Not long after, he was writhing on the floor, holding his stomach, crying, "Mommy, Mommy, Mommy! I'm sorry, I'm sorry, I know I ate too many cookies, I'll never do it again—just make it stop hurting!" Pain has a powerful effect, and God has the grace to use our pain for our good if we're ready to listen to him.

I yielded to God amid pain in my own life. I grew up in a close-knit family. We did everything together. My dad was actively involved in my life—it was wonderful. But when I was fourteen, my parents divorced, and my dad moved out. My stable world was shaken.

I remember one particular night when my father visited. My mother was telling him that he needed to help us kids, and I got in the middle of it. I had a bad argument with my dad, and he disciplined me—actually, he punched me. Then he left to go wherever he was living at the time. I went to my room, sobbing. It was the worst pain I'd ever felt in my life.

Hanging above my stereo was a pencil sketch of Jesus that I had drawn. I remember looking at the picture and crying out to God. I was in such emotional pain that I could only say two words: "God, help." It was the first and only time I heard the audible voice of God. He said, "Don't worry my son; it will be okay." The hairs on the back of my neck stood up; the moment was surreal. The voice was so loud that I jumped and turned around, looking to see who was standing behind me. But no one was in the room except me—and God. From that moment on, I really, really knew that the source of my strength was God.

I don't want to diminish the impact of that time—it was unbelievably painful for me and my family. If you had walked into our house at that time and peeked into our bedrooms, you would have found us all teary-eyed and feeling alone. But you also would have found each of us reading the Bible. Because of all the pain in our lives, my family was driven to church.

During that time, I pressed in hard to God, looking to him for strength. And because that pain drove me to God and caused me to surrender to him, I discovered my calling to ministry. The pastor of our church saw the pain in our lives and my desire to yield to God in the midst of it. He took me under his wing and discipled me, teaching me about God and helping me discover and yield to God's purpose for my life. I worked as a volunteer youth leader, then as a volunteer youth minister. That same pastor asked me, at the age of nineteen, to preach my first sermon at one of the Sunday-night services—a sermon for adults.

I remember that moment like it was yesterday; I was preaching in a school auditorium, on an elevated platform that served the school as a stage. The people were sitting on folded chairs, and as I spoke, I felt as if I could walk off that stage and not fall—that I could walk on the air above the crowd. Through that feeling I knew God was saying to me, *"This is what I've called you to do."* It was the greatest sense of euphoria I've ever experienced. And I knew then that this was what I would do for the rest of my life.

God used the pain of my parents' divorce to bring my family closer to him. He used that pain to speak personally to me, and he used that pain to lead me to the great and wonderful purpose he had planned for my life.

Seven years after their divorce, my parents got married again—to each other. As I write this book, they've been together this time for fifteen years. God can use pain for our great good, and he can heal our pain too. My family and I are living proof.

So was the apostle Paul. After God grabbed his attention, Saul spent three days waiting in the house of a stranger in Damascus, completely blind, neither eating nor drinking. But you can bet he was listening—and yielding himself to God's new plan for his life.

You can bet in that darkness, in that strange, pagan city, Saul was wondering what God was going to say next. Wouldn't you be? I know I would! And for three days, God let Saul's pain linger. Like the hunter with the young eagle, God left Saul sitting in the dark, disoriented and hungry. Saul was being tuned to hear the voice of the Master over the voice of the self-righteous Pharisee who had stormed out of Jerusalem, convinced he knew what God wanted and how to handle those who disagreed. Suddenly Saul discovered that everything he had relied upon—his studies, his upbringing, his position, his authority—were worthless. He was alone, he was hungry, and he was blind. Rather than relying on himself, he suddenly had to rely on God utterly and completely. He chose to yield completely to God. He was ready to switch to the right road.

That's the power of pain.

ROAD SIGN #3: TURN RIGHT

After we've stopped and yielded to God, the next step in finding the right road is to turn right. God spoke to Saul on the road to Damascus and gave him instructions to follow. But it's no surprise that those instructions led Saul to a person—someone flesh and blood, like Saul, who would guide him on his next steps toward the right path. God's standard operating procedure involves other people helping us make the right turns to get us back to God's road. In Saul's case, the first person God used was Ananias. Let's look at this part of the story:

> In Damascus there was a disciple named Ananias. The Lord called to him in a vision, "Ananias!"
>
> "Yes, Lord," he answered.
>
> The Lord told him, "Go to the house of Judas on Straight Street and ask for a man from Tarsus named Saul, for he is praying. In a

vision he has seen a man named Ananias come and place his hands on him to restore his sight."[14]

Let's stop there. You can imagine Ananias at that moment, can't you? Here he is, hiding out in Damascus from the religious authorities in Jerusalem, and God is telling him to go visit the fanatic prosecuting attorney who has already imprisoned or killed many of Ananias's friends! I'd be saying, "God? Are you sure about this? Don't you want to rethink that just a little? Maybe?" I'll bet Ananias would have preferred to say a prayer and leave an encouraging note on Saul's Facebook page!

In fact, Ananias said something of the sort:

" 'Lord,' Ananias answered, 'I have heard many reports about this man and all the harm he has done to your saints in Jerusalem. And he has come here with authority from the chief priests to arrest all who call on your name' "[15]

But God told Ananias to go anyway—and Ananias obeyed.

Then Ananias went to the house and entered it. Placing his hands on Saul, he said, "Brother Saul, the Lord—Jesus, who appeared to you on the road as you were coming here—has sent me so that you may see again and be filled with the Holy Spirit." Immediately, something like scales fell from Saul's eyes, and he could see again. He got up and was baptized, and after taking some food, he regained his strength.

Saul spent several days with the disciples in Damascus. At once he began to preach in the synagogues that Jesus is the Son of God. All those who heard him were astonished and asked, "Isn't he the man who raised havoc in Jerusalem among those who call on this name? And hasn't he come here to take them as prisoners to the chief priests?" Yet Saul grew more and more powerful and baffled the Jews living in Damascus by proving that Jesus is the Christ.[16]

Perhaps Ananias was one of the key reasons the other disciples in Damascus accepted their former persecutor into their ranks. Ananias was an example for others then and an example for us today as well. We all need an Ananias in our lives—a caring friend who will even take personal risks to help us. God uses people to help people. Paul needed Ananias, Elijah needed Elisha, Moses needed Joshua, and David needed Jonathan. And Paul himself later became an Ananias for Timothy, motivating him, encouraging him, and helping to build him into one of the great leaders of the faith.

God sent more than one person to encourage Paul and help him make the right turns to arrive at the divine destiny God intended for him. A man named Joseph was a Levite: the Levites devoted their lives to service in God's temple as assistants to the chief priests, musicians at worship, doorkeepers, or temple guards. It was an exciting dedication—something to which Levites generally looked forward. But Joseph had never been given that opportunity because he was from Cyprus, raised among Jews who had been exiled from Israel and resettled on that island.

As Joseph grew older, he made his way back to the homeland, where he was known as a Hellenist—a Greek-speaking Jew who had been brought up outside of Israel. Considerable hostility existed between the homeland Jews and the Hellenists, who had often been influenced by foreign ways and whom the homeland Jews considered to be less devout.

Joseph could have been offended and put off by the injustice and discrimination to which he was subjected, but there was no guile in his character. So unselfish and committed to helping other believers was he that at one point he sold a field he owned and gave all of the money to the disciples to help those in need.[17] His helpful, supportive nature gained him a reputation among the disciples, who nicknamed him *Barnabas*, which means Son of Encouragement.

Although Barnabas is not as well known as the apostle Paul, in a sense he had an important part in the writing of the many New Testament books Paul wrote—because it was Barnabas who encouraged Paul! After Saul's conversion, at first no one would accept him because of his past. After all, he had been a relentless persecutor who had killed Christians. Many couldn't forgive him for what he had done; others doubted that his conversion was genuine.

The book of Acts tells us that when other disciples were afraid of Paul and didn't trust him, Barnabas spoke up on his behalf. And when, in an ironic twist of events, angry Jews sought to kill Saul for his new faith in and testimony about Jesus, causing Saul to flee first to Jerusalem and then to Tarsus, Barnabas continued to be a guide and encourager for Saul as he found his way on this new road. From Antioch, Barnabas deliberately sought him out, traveling to Tarsus to find him and bring him back to Antioch to work with him in ministry. The mature, practiced believer took the new kid under his wing and walked with him on this new road of following God's will. In other words, if it hadn't been for Barnabas's intercession and encouragement, there might never have been an apostle Paul!

We all need an Ananias and could use a Barnabas in our lives to help us make the right turns to arrive at the divine destiny God intends for us. We can also be such encouragers for others as they turn their lives around. Recently, during my prayer time, I felt that God wanted me to pray for a young woman who is part of our church's worship team. I knew of no reason for this impulse, but I immediately prayed for her and thanked God for her talent and her work for the church. When I was done, I posted a note on her Facebook page, telling her that God had put it on my heart to pray for her and to thank her personally for her efforts with our worship team. Only a few minutes went by before she phoned me.

"Pastor," she said, "You won't believe this, but I had been having a lot of doubts lately, and yesterday I asked God to confirm that he wanted me to continue with the worship team. And this morning, I got your message!"

God stopped Saul when he was heading down the wrong road. Moved by the agent of pain, Saul yielded to God. Then God used people—like Ananias and Barnabas—to help turn Saul onto the right path for his life. They encouraged him, guided him, and were living examples of what Saul could be with God's help. Partly through the influence of those men, God changed Saul from a murderous zealot into perhaps the most powerful witness for God in the history of the church. That's the power of encouragement from the people God puts in our lives.

ROAD SIGN #4: GO!

Once we've stopped going down the wrong road, yielded ourselves to God, and turned to follow God with the encouragement and guidance of caring friends, how can we find and follow that specific road that is God's will for our lives? That's when God gives us the fourth road sign: "Go!"

God won't leave us without direction and guidance. In fact, looking back, we can see that he was directing us and trying to help us all along, even when we were fighting against it and going our own way. Take a look at Saul's question and Jesus' reply on the road to Damascus:

> He said, "Who are You, Lord?"
> Then the Lord said, "I am Jesus, whom you are persecuting. It is hard for you to kick against the goads."[18]

What are goads? Goads are sharp, pointed sticks used to get oxen moving and guide them in the right direction. What's an ox? One of the most stubborn animals on the planet. (Small wonder that God compares us to oxen.) You might rightly note that kicking against a sharp, pointed stick would hurt the kicker, not the stick.

One definition of *goad* is "something that urges or stimulates into action."[19] When Saul was on the wrong road, God was there urging or stimulating him to stop, yield, and turn in the right direction. That's good news for every person who wonders how on earth he or she will ever be able to discern God's direction for his or her life. God doesn't leave us without guidance. He's always goading, directing, nudging us down the path to his perfect will for our lives. God's prodding may be dramatic, as it was with Saul, or it may be more subtle: he often guides us through our inner compasses—in other words, our instincts. Our gut feelings and intuitions can be God speaking in our hearts—if we stop kicking against the goads and yield ourselves, truly desiring to follow him. That still small voice in our hearts can be the most important element in helping us to step out in confidence and take the road God has called us to travel.

I'll share a story of when I followed God's nudging in my own ministry. At that time our staff members were examining our worship ministry, particularly the musical element of our service. We felt we needed to upgrade the quality, we wanted to start a gospel choir, and we wanted to find the right worship pastor for our ministry. Not long before this, we had invited a well-known worship-music recording artist to sing at our church. I'd always been a big fan of his music, and when he came, he and I got to know each other. We hit it off and had a great time.

Now, I love to worship in the morning while getting ready for my day. I'll play a CD of worship music and sing along as I shower and get dressed. When I played my new friend's CD—enjoying the music, worshipping God—inside. I felt God telling me: *"Call him and ask if he'll come on staff and help take your worship ministry to the next level."* But I just thought, *Wow, sure. Anyone would want him to come. That's just my head.* So I ignored it.

But over the next few days, whenever I listened to music in the morning, I would get that same inner feeling nudging me to make the call. Finally I gave in—but first I consulted with some trusted advisors, because the last thing I wanted was to come across as a spiritual nut job. They laughed but reassured me that if I thought the Lord was leading me to make the call, I should make the call.

So I did. Right off the bat, I told the artist, "Look, this is going to sound bizarre. I never say God is leading me to do something, because I know it can come across as flaky. And if it's bizarre to you, you don't have to be polite; you can just say, 'No, I don't feel like this is God.' But would you be willing to come be our worship pastor and help us with our worship ministry?"

There was a slight pause, during which I was certain I had just achieved spiritual-nut-job status. But then he said, "Well, it's funny you're asking me this question. About a month ago someone (he named a prominent minister) asked me if I'd be on his staff, but I really didn't feel like it was God. Just two weeks ago, someone else (he named an even more prominent minister) called and asked the same thing. But I didn't feel that was God."

At this point I'm thinking, *Well, if those guys weren't from God, what are my chances?*

But then he continued: "But I'd really like to sit down and talk with you about it, because I feel this might be God."

Chills went through me. To make a long story short, he did come and help us build our worship ministry, working with us for about a year and a half to start a gospel choir and select a worship pastor. The experience of working with him also began a long, close friendship that continues today. And it all happened because I was willing to trust that inner voice—to listen to God's nudging.

God's final road sign is "Go!" He wants us to step out in a new direction, following his leading. We can go in confidence when we don't kick against the goads but instead follow his nudging. But many of us fear we'll make the wrong path decision; we don't trust that what we're feeling or hearing in our hearts is truly from God. We've made bad decisions in the past because of our limited wisdom and knowledge, which frequently prove to be faulty. So how can we be sure we're listing to God's voice and not our own?

Solomon provides us with sound advice concerning how to overcome this limitation. When he was still very young, Solomon became king and was given the responsibility of rebuilding the temple. God appeared to him in a dream and said, basically, "Ask anything you want, and I'll give it to you—long life, lots of money, the destruction of all your enemies, or whatever else you might want."

Solomon replied: "Here's what I want: Give me a God-listening heart so I can lead your people well, discerning the difference between good and evil. For who on their own is capable of leading your glorious people?"[20] He had the right idea: none of us is capable of accomplishing God's will for our lives without a "God-listening heart."

God's response to Solomon's humble request was to tell him, in essence, "Since you haven't asked for any of the material things I mentioned, I'll give you all of them anyway, and I will also give you the wisdom you asked for. There will never be anyone like you in all the world—you'll be the wisest man who has ever lived."[21]

Even after becoming the wisest man who ever lived, Solomon still admonished us to "trust in the LORD with all your heart and lean not on your own understanding; in all your ways acknowledge him, and he will make your paths straight. Do not be wise in your own eyes."[22]

Solomon's example illustrates that it's not the gathering of more information that enables us to make the right path choices. Relying on our own wisdom doesn't enable us to make the right path choices. Only trusting in the Lord's guidance truly enables us to make the right path choices. When we consult God, when we ask him what path he would have us take, that's when we get on the right road; that's when our paths are made straight. Submission to God's will always leads us in the right direction.

Too often, we think trusting in the Lord and submitting to his will only has to do with spiritual things. We think it means, "Trust in the Lord when you go to prayer time. Trust in the Lord when you're reading the Bible." But we don't realize that we should trust in the Lord and lean not on our own understanding when it comes to everyday decisions of life. "All your ways" means all your ways— dating, marriage, occupation, education, even entertainment. We should turn to God when we decide whom to date, whom to marry, what career path to take. We should turn to him when we choose where to go for our education and what we should major in. We should trust God about whom we should allow to be our close friends. In the everyday things we all experience. In *all* your ways, not *some* of your ways—not compartments in your life but *in everything you do*, lean on God's understanding and not on your own.

Trusting in the Lord was something I had to learn in my own life. Throughout high school I dated the same girl. While I was dating her, I felt the Lord telling me over and over again that she was not the right person for me. She wasn't a Christian, and although I was, I certainly couldn't claim that I was behaving like one. Nobody who saw me would have known I was a Christian. Even though I had made that choice, I wasn't living the life. Yet God kept nudging me over and over again that she wasn't the one, that if I was going to be serious with him, I needed to trust him to bring the right woman into my life.

When I was nineteen years old, in the summer between high school and college, I was at a crossroads. Finally, I said, "Okay, God, I'm willing to give her up. I'm willing to let you take her out of my life." And sure enough, through a series of events, he did. So I said, "Okay, Lord, I'm going to trust you in my dating and my marriage. I trust you to bring somebody into my life who loves you, who fits what you want in a wife for me."

About ten months after this, when I was getting involved in the church youth group and starting to be a leader, God brought a young woman into that church who began helping with the youth group as a fellow leader. Working together, we formed a relationship that was based on the principles of God's Word. It began as a friendship and, with the blessing of God, flourished into a marriage. Because I was willing to trust in the Lord's ways rather than my own, I wound up meeting the woman God had chosen for me to spend the rest of my life with.

How do we submit to God? How do we know which path God wants us to take? The answer is that we must pay attention to the goads. Heed the inner promptings God is giving us. Listen to and follow the feelings that are shouting at us, saying, *"This is wrong, don't do it!"* or, *"Yes, go for it! I'm behind you!"*

That's exactly what Saul eventually did. When Jesus told Saul that it was hard for him to "kick against the goads," he meant that up to that point Saul had been ignoring God's nudgings. He'd been going against the inner voice that had been telling him that he was fighting against truth and was on the wrong path. Resistance had been difficult for Saul because God, as he always is, had been relentless with his goads; but now it was time for Saul to listen to a wisdom that was not his own. It was time to stop leaning solely on his own understanding and to listen to and put his trust in God.

When Saul stopped kicking against the goads and yielded to God, Jesus told him to go to Straight Street in Damascus and wait for a man named Ananias, who would bring healing to his eyes and set him on the right path. I love the fact that Jesus sent Saul to the "Straight" Street, as if to echo the promise from Proverbs: "Trust in the LORD with all your heart and lean not on your own understanding; in all your ways acknowledge him, and he will make your paths straight" (3:5–6).

God took Saul's life, which had been disastrously headed down the wrong road, and completely turned it around, transforming him from a callous and coldhearted enemy of the faith into the most ardent proponent of the gospel that the world has ever known! And when you're headed down the wrong road in your life, God can work a miraculous change in you.

3

MOVING FORWARD AFTER
YOU'VE BLOWN IT

Like many teenage boys, I developed an expensive habit—a girl-friend. I liked to take my girlfriend out to nice places, and sometimes I didn't have the money to do so. But I knew where to find it. At the time, my mother kept a stack of hundred dollar bills in her armoire. This stack of bills was huge—it must have been five to seven inches thick; she probably had $10,000 or more in that stack. One day my mother sent me up to get something out of her drawer, and I saw that stack of bills for the first time. I thought, *Wow! I need a hundred bucks for tonight.* So I took a hundred-dollar bill.

About a week or two went by, and my mother never said anything. I was expecting her to say, "Hey, I had ten thousand dollars there, how come I only have nine thousand nine hundred there now?" So I thought since she didn't notice that I'd taken one of the bills, I might as well take another. Soon just about every week for four months, I'd go into her room and take a hundred-dollar bill—sometimes I'd take two. My girlfriend and I were going to some very nice places.

But then I decided to get serious with God, to truly give my heart fully to Christ—and one of the first things Christ talked to me about was that money. He said, *"You need to tell your mother you took all that money."* I started thinking about it and realized that by the time it was all said and done, I must have taken several thousand dollars—just flat out stolen it—from my mother. I had blown it, big time.

I went to my mother and said, "Mom, I need to tell you something. I've committed my life to Christ, and I feel like I need to be honest with you." Here it came—deep breath—"I've been stealing money from you for the last four months. You know the stack of hundreds you have up there in your drawer? I've been taking that money."

I was ready for anything—ready for her to yell at me, to ground me, ready for any punishment she could dream up. I deserved it, and I knew it.

But my mother just said, "I'm disappointed in you, Frank, but I'm happy that you told me. I completely forgive you."

And that was it.

I was stunned. "Don't you want me to pay it back?"

"No," she said, "you don't have to pay it back. I appreciate that you came and told me, and all is forgiven."

God's Unconditional Love for Us

My mother's reaction was a nearly perfect replica of God's reaction to us when we've blown it. She forgave me, unconditionally, on the spot. And you know what? Not that she intended this, but her goodness and kindness in dealing with me made me feel more sorrowful than if she'd punished me. I was ready for punishment—I wasn't ready for forgiveness.

At one time or another, everyone has blown it, is blowing it, or will blow it. So it's comforting to know that God can and wants to turn our lives around even after we've blown it. Perhaps best of all, it's good to know that when we blow it, God still loves us.

This paraphrase of Romans 8:31–39 from *The Message* offers a succinct affirmation of God's love and caring:

So, what do you think? With God on our side like this, how can we lose? If God didn't hesitate to put everything on the line for us, embracing our condition and exposing himself to the worst by sending his own Son, is there anything else he wouldn't gladly and freely do for us? And who would dare tangle with God by messing with one of God's chosen? Who would dare even to point a finger? The One who died for us—who was raised to life for us!—is in the presence of God at this very moment sticking up for us. Do you think anyone is going to be able to drive a wedge between us and Christ's love for us? There is no way! Not trouble, not hard times, not hatred, not hunger, not homelessness, not bullying threats, not backstabbing, not even the worst sins listed in Scripture:

They kill us in cold blood because they hate you.

We're sitting ducks; they pick us off one by one.

None of this fazes us because Jesus loves us. I'm absolutely convinced that nothing—nothing living or dead, angelic or demonic, today or tomorrow, high or low, thinkable or unthinkable—absolutely nothing can get between us and God's love because of the way that Jesus our Master has embraced us.

God's Word tells us that even after we've blown it, he loves us and wants to turn our lives around! That when we've blown it, God still wants to use us. That when we've blown it, God is still committed to us. That when we've blown it, God still has wonderful plans for our lives.

Why We Think We've Blown Our Chances with God

As true as it is that God loves us no matter what we've done or how we've goofed up, most of us have a hard time believing it. What are the reasons we think we no longer merit God's love or qualify for his blessings and calling on our lives? I'd like to explore three.

1. WE FORGET WE'RE CHRONICALLY HUMAN

Here's how Dieter Zander, teaching pastor at Willow Creek Community Church, puts it:

> If the following signs are observed, I am not emotionally disturbed or dying. If you find me stumbling and falling, I may be trying something new. I am learning.
>
> If you find me sad, I may have realized that I have been making the same mistakes again and again. I am exploring. If you find me frightened, I may be in a new situation. I am reaching out. If you find me crying, I may have failed. I am lonely. If you find me being very quiet, I may be planning. I am trying again.
>
> These are all life signs of beings of my nature. If prolonged absence of the above indicators is observed, do not perform an autopsy. First, provide an opportunity and invitation for life to emerge because I am chronically human.[1]

Everyone has faults and failings. No one is exempt from having bad days. Everyone has doubts, we all struggle with pride from time to time, and all of us have secrets of which we're ashamed. Let's face it: we all are chronically human, so we have a hard time believing that after we've blown it for the hundredth time, God still wants to turn our lives around. But the truth is, God loves to turn around the lives of those who have blown it!

2. WE'RE IMPRISONED BY THE PAST

The second reason it's hard for us to believe that God can turn our lives around even when we've blown it is that we put ourselves in a prison of our own making, held captive by our past experiences. When we blow it, our sense of guilt allows the past to dog us forever. After all, haven't we all wished, like poet Louisa Fletcher, for

some wonderful place
Called the Land of Beginning Again,
Where all our mistakes and all our heartaches
And all of our poor, selfish grief
Could be dropped, like a shabby old coat, at the door,
*And never put on again.*²

Wouldn't you love to do that—just drop every mistake you've made down on the floor and walk into a new life, knowing you'd never hear about them again? People the world over have a basic desire for Fletcher's Land of Beginning Again. We even have terms for it—you may have used some of them yourself: a fresh start, a second chance, a clean slate, a mulligan, a do-over. We talk about such opportunities, dream about them, wistfully long for them—but how often do we actually let go and accept that second chance? Instead of dropping the shabby old coat, we drag it along with us.

Fortunately, God knows how destructive hanging on to the past can be, so he admonishes us to forget those things that are behind us and focus intently on what lies ahead.³

A local story in the Northeast illustrates the need for letting go of the past—particularly of the things that hold us back. Our area boasts a large Puerto Rican population with a rich culture and heritage. As in many cultures, the Puerto Ricans have unique spices and sauces that give their food distinctive flavors. One of these sauces is called *sofrito*—a mixture of vegetables and spices used as a base to flavor meats, rice, beans, and just about everything else.

About thirty years ago, the owner of a *bodega*—a small grocery store catering to the Puerto Rican population—started making his own sofrito. He served it to family and friends, who raved about how good it was. He eventually shared some with his pastor, who is a friend of mine, and his pastor encouraged him to start selling it as a product. But the man was afraid of the risk. He worried that if he spent his time making the sofrito, his little grocery store would suffer and he would lose his livelihood. Everyone told him, "You need to sell this, it's good!" But he dragged his feet, held back by his little bodega.

Finally he decided to take a small risk and sell the sofrito at his store. It became an instant hit. Today his recipe is the top-selling sofrito in the Northeast. I have a staff member who drives to New Haven once a month to stock up on this sofrito, because his wife won't cook with any other brand. Today all the man's family does is manufacture the sofrito, an extremely lucrative venture. As for the little bodega the man was so afraid to lose—he wound up selling it because it took time away from his making the sofrito!

Like the man and his bodega, forgetting what is behind us is an important step toward allowing God to turn our lives around. Experiencing a turnaround means looking to the future, not the past.

The apostle Paul understood that well. His past was filled with pain, sin, and numerous mistakes. He'd done many things that were reprehensible and dead wrong. He knew he would have to let go of the past if he was to live fruitfully in the present and make tomorrow better.

Like Paul, if we're going to experience a turnaround in our lives, we have to move on, remembering that with God's help we can move triumphantly beyond all our mistakes and heartaches—to a real Land of Beginning Again. We can begin finding our way to that destination the moment we decide to accept God's forgiveness and step out of the prison of our past problems.

3. WE'RE BLINDED BY THE PAST

We must choose not to make the same mistake as the Peanuts cartoon character Lucy. In one cartoon strip, outfielder Lucy, who almost never seems to catch a fly ball, misses yet another easy out.

Explaining her error to Charlie Brown, she says, "I started thinking about all the other balls I missed. The past got in my eyes."

That's what happens to many of us. The past gets in our eyes for a variety of reasons.

First, we too often base our self-worth on the things we do—both the good and the bad. Many of us have such a poor sense of self-worth that we're convinced any mistake we make is just one more bit of proof that we're worthless. We overreact, telling ourselves that we're stupid and that what we've done is just further evidence that we're losers who are doomed to fail repeatedly.

An old story about two water pots illustrates how we can put our past misjudgments and mistakes in perspective and not allow them to distort our feelings of self-worth.

Once upon a time in India, there lived a water bearer. It was his job to supply his village with water from the river. He carried across his neck two large pots hung on either end of a long pole. Both pots were large and should have been able to carry much water for the village. But one pot had a small crack in it, so as the bearer walked along, water would trickle out. By the time he reached the village, the cracked pot would be half empty, while the perfect pot was still filled to the brim. The bearer had to make multiple trips to the river to carry enough water for the village. At night the perfect pot would boast of its fine service for their master and the village, carrying a full load of water with every trip. But the cracked pot would sit silently in shame.

For two years the cracked pot felt the water seep away, knowing each day it could not do the work for which it was intended. At last, one morning when they reached the river, the pot cried out to its master in anguish. "O, master! I am ashamed!"

The water bearer, unsurprised to hear a talking pot, simply replied, "Why are you ashamed?"

"Because for two years you have used me to carry water from the river, but I have not served you well. I have a crack, and I have spilled the water the village needs along the path, making you take many trips. You should replace me with a better pot; I am good for nothing!"

The water bearer smiled. "If that is what you wish. But first, serve me but one more time. And as we walk back to the village, tell me what you see."

So the water bearer filled the two pots and carried them, as before, back to the village. The cracked pot obeyed its master, looking to see what it could. But all it could see was the dusty path and the many colorful flowers that grew along it. There was nothing else. And the whole way, the water continued to trickle from the pot.

"What did you see?" asked the water bearer when they reached the village.

"Oh, master, I saw nothing but the path and the flowers and my water pouring out," replied the cracked pot sadly.

"Were the flowers beautiful?"

"Oh yes, they were lovely, master. I thank you for the sight. The flowers did make me feel better. But still, I have done you very poor service, and I should not be your pot."

The master smiled. "Tell me, my good pot, did you see any flowers on the other side of the path?"

The pot thought a moment and replied, "No, master, all I saw was the dust of India."

His master nodded. "I have known about your crack from the moment I chose you. I planted seeds along your side of the path, so that you might water them as I walked. Because of you, our village has flowers to brighten our homes, the young girls wear flowers in their hair, and even the poorest bride may celebrate her wedding day covered in the colors of a princess."[4]

Like the cracked pot, we are all flawed. But so many of us spend our time concentrating on our flaws, focusing on each little mistake, each little spill of water, that we fail to see what our Master is doing through us. Regardless of our flaws—few or many, little or big—in God's hands we are still of great value. So don't let your perceived imperfections distort your opinion of yourself and imprison you.

The truth is that our value comes not from what we do but from who—or rather whose—we are. In Luke 20:20–26, when a crowd questioned Jesus about the need to pay taxes to Caesar, Jesus responded that the coin they showed him belonged to Caesar, as evidenced by Caesar's image imprinted on the face of the coin. In the same way, all of us have the imprint of God on us because we were made in his image. God's imprint is on us, showing that we belong to him. It is that imprint that gives us our value. It doesn't come from what we do right or what we do wrong; it comes from God's mark on our lives.

Second, we mistakenly believe that wrongs deserve to be punished forever. As a consequence, we have a hard time forgiving ourselves, so we go into self-flagellation mode and flog ourselves again and again.

- We flog ourselves because of the regrettable way we've raised our children—and go through life feeling like failed parents.
- We flog ourselves over the shame of having inappropriate relationships—and live under that guilt forever.
- We flog ourselves over being part of marriages that failed—and live with the regret of not having done something differently.

Whatever we perceive to be the cause, many of us languish under an oppressive weight of guilt, shame, and regret over something for which we can't forgive ourselves, stuck in the memory of yesterday and blocked from moving forward because the past is in our eyes. Making matters even worse, we punish ourselves in all sorts of ways for past mistakes. Maybe we don't allow ourselves to laugh, get close to anyone, or receive anything good in life because we think our past mistakes make us unworthy of anything better, especially when we've really blown it big time. But when we refuse to forgive ourselves, we make our own standard of forgiveness higher than God's—in essence, we make ourselves bigger than God!

In the Old Testament, an imperfect person had to bring a perfect lamb to the priest in order to be forgiven. The priest would inspect the lamb to see if it was without spot or blemish; if the lamb was perfect, the man was forgiven. Notice that it was a given that the man was imperfect—his forgiveness was dependent on the inspection of the lamb. If the priest viewed the lamb as perfect, the man was automatically forgiven, even though he was imperfect.

That's the same way it works today. When you and I come to God with our sin, God inspects the Lamb—his Son—and because *Christ* is perfect, *we* are forgiven. But when we don't forgive ourselves, we're saying that our standard of forgiveness is greater than God's standard of forgiveness. We're almost slapping God in the face. He sacrificed his Son, who is that perfect Lamb, and we're saying, "That's just not good enough."

Third, we misunderstand just how different God's forgiveness is from human forgiveness. As a result, we often struggle to accept God's forgiveness, still allowing the past to blind us. People often hold on to their feelings of guilt; but God forgives and forgets, promising us that he will remember our sins no more.[5]

People like to set rules for forgiveness—"I'll forgive you if . . ." But God tells us that we only need to ask. People try to make us feel ashamed when we ask for forgiveness, but God will embrace us and affirm our worth. His forgiveness is so far above human forgiveness that he even goes so far as to destroy the record of our wrongdoing.[6]

Do you remember that even after Peter denied Jesus three times the night of Jesus' crucifixion, the risen Jesus later appeared to him and asked: "Peter, do you love me?" Ashamed of what he had done, Peter was wounded by Jesus' question, which Jesus repeated three times. Perhaps Peter believed that he was being rebuked for his treachery. So, in sorrowful frustration, Peter answered Jesus, "Lord, you know all things; you know that I love you" (John 21:17).

But Jesus wasn't rebuking Peter or trying to leave him paralyzed in the memory of his past mistake. He was offering Peter a chance to redeem himself, erasing the heavenly record of his treachery and—in three declarations of Peter's love for him—forgiving Peter for denying him each of those three times.

God is often more forgiving of us than we are of ourselves. If you've asked God to forgive you, and you really mean it, he has forgiven you. So accept his forgiveness and move forward. Don't listen to those voices of self-recrimination: they're not from God. He delights in forgiving you and wiping away the bitterness of the past, and he'll help you turn your life around.

Finally, we allow ourselves to be overcome by regrets that tempt us to give up, fearing that we'll never get another opportunity like the one we've blown. We think we'll never find another job like the one we lost, never be able to repair our marriage, never meet another person like the one who "got away." We tell ourselves we can't possibly make up for what we've done. We become mired in an endless cycle of regret and recrimination.

When we've blown it, all sorts of negative thoughts about ourselves and our lives can stand in our way and block our progress. Remember, though, that all we need to do is call to mind God's promise of Romans 8:28—"In all things God works for the good of those who love him." We can be assured that, regardless of the bad things we've done or the opportunities we've missed along the way, God can make something positive out of all of it. He can turn our lives around and put us on a new path toward success and fulfillment even after we've blown it. No matter what we've done, God can give us a new direction and a new life!

The Long Road Back

God has a long history of turning around lives after people have blown it. Let me remind you of the Bible story of a man, Moses, whose life God turned around after he had really blown it—not just a little, but in a really dramatic way.

Moses was born to Hebrew slaves in Egypt (at that time, all of the Hebrews were slaves). Pharaoh, the ruler of Egypt, worried that the Hebrew population was growing faster than the native Egyptians. Fearing a slave revolt, he ordered the midwives to kill any male Hebrew babies.[7] So Moses' mother put him in a tiny boat and hid it among the bulrushes in the Nile. Pharaoh's daughter found the baby and adopted him, giving him a life of privilege and education that no Hebrew could otherwise have hoped for. This son of a slave was now a prince of the royal family![8]

Jump ahead forty years. Moses has everything. He's educated. He's rich. He's the adopted grandson of Pharaoh, perhaps in line to become a pharaoh himself. In the *Who's Who* list of Egypt, Moses is pretty close to the top. But one day he took a walk to where his own people, the Hebrew slaves, were hard at labor. He watched them making bricks while Egyptian guards beat them with whips. Moses felt an overwhelming compassion for his people—he identified with the Hebrew people rather than their overlords, the Egyptians. Perhaps it pained him to watch them trying to rest for a moment from their labors, only to be whipped and forced to work harder. When he saw an Egyptian savagely beating one of his people, he faced a life-altering decision. He had to decide whether to protect himself or be true to his heart and try to protect his downtrodden countryman—to risk his comfort, his position, his reputation—to risk everything by coming to the rescue of his people. If he ignored his heart, he would continue to enjoy all the privileges to which he had become accustomed.

The Bible tells us: "He looked this way and that way, and when he saw no one, he killed the Egyptian and hid him in the sand" (Exodus 2:12 NKJV).

Notice that he looked everywhere except up. Moses was concerned about what others would think, but he forgot to consider what God would think. Whenever we choose to be people pleasers rather than God pleasers, we're almost certain to make major mistakes. Moses understood that if what he had done were discovered, his privileged life would be over.

So what did he do? Moses did what many of us first try to do after we've blown it: he tried to cover up what he'd done. He hid the Egyptian's body in the sand, perhaps reasoning that if he buried it, what he'd done would not become known. After all, Egypt was a dangerous place. Lions roamed the desert; serpents infested the reeds, and crocodiles lurked in the river. Maybe Moses hoped the other Egyptians would think the man had taken a wrong turn and became an afternoon snack. And surely the Israelite workers would understand the significance of what Moses had done for them— and appreciate it. Acts 7:25 tells us: "Moses thought that his own people would realize that God was using him to rescue them, but they did not."

Moses would soon learn that he couldn't go on living as he always had—friend of the people and son of the princess—like some caped superhero maintaining his "Bruce Wayne" identity by day while secretly fighting oppression in the shadows.

Moses' heart was right: but his method—murder—was not only not in God's plan, it was a horrible mistake. In trying to do a good thing in his own power and his own way, Moses had blown it big time. Did Moses' rash act disqualify him forever from being the deliverer of his people that he thought God had destined him to be?

Hardly. Remember, God delights in turning our lives around after we've blown it. Moses' life is an excellent example of the three steps God uses to do just that.

TURNAROUND STEP 1: REVEAL

Moses buried the Egyptian—and, he hoped, his problems—in the sand. But that was not to be the end of it.

> The next day he went out and saw two Hebrews fighting. He asked the one in the wrong, "Why are you hitting your fellow Hebrew?"
>
> The man said, "Who made you ruler and judge over us? Are you thinking of killing me as you killed the Egyptian?" Then Moses was afraid and thought, "What I did must have become known"[9]

God will not permit a cover-up. The first step God takes in turning our lives around after we blow it is to shock us back to reality by exposing what we've tried so hard to cover up. God loves us too much to allow us to live hiding something we've done; loves us too much to allow us to spend the rest of our lives in fear of discovery. He begins the process of turning us around by exposing what we've done.

Imagine how Moses' "mistake" may have become known. Perhaps, in his haste to cover up what he'd done, Moses didn't bury the Egyptian's body deep enough. Maybe Moses went home that evening confident he could live on both sides of the track, so to speak. But as the cool of night settled on the desert, things began to happen. The wind shifts the sand. A bird pecks at something shiny. A jackal sniffs and paws some loose ground. The morning sun rises on a body in the sand, and Moses' "mistake" is uncovered. God has been at work.

When we cover things up, we only hurt ourselves. On the outside things may look as smooth as a desert dune, but on the inside we're a boiling mess. God doesn't want us to live under a cloud of fear, guilt, and shame for the rest of our lives. He doesn't want us looking over our shoulder or living in dishonesty as we wear a false front. He wants to give us peace—real peace. And to do that, God allows what we've covered up to be uncovered—not to hurt us but to free us from the harmful, haunting effects of our misdeeds.

When Pharaoh learned what Moses had done, he tried to kill his adopted grandson,[10] likely keenly aware that Moses' actions demonstrated that his loyalties lay not with the Egyptians but with the Israelites. Moses no longer had a choice about which world he would live in—he was now an outcast from both. God's first step in the process of turning Moses' life around, shocking him by allowing his deed to be uncovered, certainly produced its intended effect. Let's go back to the scene.

Doubly tormented by the conflict in his mind between his two allegiances and by the knowledge that he had blown it, Moses was now persona non grata in both worlds. A man without a country and without friends, he had to flee Egypt.

TURNAROUND STEP 2: REFINE

Where could Moses go to escape Pharaoh's wrath? From a purely practical point of view, Moses didn't have many choices. Almost all of the territory surrounding the land of Egypt was either under Egyptian control or heavily monitored by Egypt. So he settled on Midian, an isolated desert community where little happened other than the grazing of sheep.

Moses may have thought he was just finding a place to hide, but

God's hand can be seen in the choice. Midian would be the place where God would refine Moses through years of wilderness living, the second step God would take to turn Moses' life around and prepare him for his destiny. During his forty-year exile in the wilderness, Moses would gain both knowledge and personal maturity. Midian would mold him for his eventual role as shepherd of his people, when he would lead the Israelite "flock's" exodus from Egypt. That's the power of a wilderness experience.

Now, by a wilderness experience, I don't mean camping. I'm talking about life on the outside—a time when your dreams and your reality are polar opposites. You look around you and find not one sign of success—just the shattered remains after a horrible, horrible failure. Every moment is a struggle. All your old convenient support pieces are gone. All your old friends are gone, or treat you like you have a contagious disease. You're isolated, depressed, emotionally drained, and you wonder how—or if—it's going to end.

No wonder we cringe when we think of wilderness experiences. Yet they play an essential role in refining us and preparing us for our divinely intended purpose. When God refines us in the wilderness, he uses the isolation to turn our focus to him. He uses the difficulties to wear off our rough edges, shaping our character to become more like his. Malachi 3:3 describes the process and effects of God's refining of the nation of Israel: "He [God] will sit as a refiner and purifier of silver; he will purify the Levites and refine them like gold and silver. Then the LORD will have men who will bring offerings in righteousness."

Before raw silver can be fashioned into jewelry or tableware, it must be refined. Impure silver will produce a flawed product of little value. So all the natural impurities that mar it must be removed. The silversmith begins the refining process by holding the silver in a crucible over a hot fire, keeping the refining bowl in the center of the flames. Here the temperature is the highest, and as the silver melts, the impurities, or dross, rise to the surface and are burned away by the heat.

The refiner must watch the molten silver carefully during the entire process. If it remains in the fire too long, it will oxidize and be difficult to work, even unusable. Fortunately, at the crucial moment of purity, molten silver develops a mirror-like finish. The refiner knows the silver is pure and ready to be used when he sees his own image reflected in it.[11]

Why must we sometimes spend time in the wilderness? To burn out our impurities. But God is watching us the whole time—even when the fires of life are their hottest—ready to pull us from the heat when at last our dross is burned away and we reflect his image.

God began refining Moses' character the very day he arrived in Midian's desert. The fugitive sat down by a well to drink and rest, and seven young women came to the well to water their flock of sheep. As Moses watched, a band of shepherds came along who began harassing the girls, driving them away from the well to claim the water—a rare commodity in the region—for their own flocks. Although Moses had plenty of his own worries, he immediately went to the girls' aid, single-handedly driving off the shepherds.

Because of this Egyptian stranger's heroics, it seems the girls made it home in record time. Surprised at their early return, their father, Jethro, a Midianite priest,[12] sought out their rescuer and invited him to dinner. Jethro took the new arrival under his wing and gave him a job as tender of his sheep—a job Moses held during his entire stay in Midian. Imagine what an adjustment this must have been for Moses: he went from being part of Egypt's royal court to being a humble shepherd in a desolate wilderness.

Sometime later, Moses married Zipporah, one of Jethro's daughters (who had likely taken special notice of the handsome rescuer at the well). Jethro also was known as Reuel, meaning "friend of God," which indicates he was not the typical pagan priest Moses would have known in Egypt, but rather a priest of God. What a providential guide Jethro must have been to his new son-in-law! Away from the influence of the palace and the countless false gods of Egypt, Moses could more fully learn about the one true God, the God of his forefathers and his people. Later in Exodus, Jethro appears as a mentor to Moses, guiding him with godly advice in the task of leading the Israelites.[13] Undoubtedly, that guidance had begun in Midian, where God began Moses' refining process.

When we've blown it, we may find ourselves in the wilderness, as Moses did. We may feel as if the time spent there is equivalent to serving time in a prison of our own making—in punishment for our sin. Or we may feel irrelevant, relegated to the sideline, with little purpose left in life. But I challenge you to see your time in the wilderness as a time for God to refine you, purify you, and prepare you for the next step. Use your time in the wilderness to press in close to God. Learn about him, love him, and allow him to shape you and ready you for the next phase in turning your life around.

TURNAROUND STEP 3: RECOMMISSION

Jump ahead another forty years. Moses—now a married man with two sons—didn't yet realize it, but his time in the wilderness was about to be over. God had burned away his impurities of pride and self-reliance. Moses, once educated by the greatest minds of pagan Egypt, has now learned about the one God from a wise old country priest. Moses, once a prince with servants at his command, has willingly served another without complaint for years on end. Now, when the Refiner looked into Moses' heart, he saw his own image.

Moses was ready for God's next step in turning his life around: recommissioning. On Horeb, the mountain of God, Moses would hear from God personally—and be commissioned for the special task for which Moses was now uniquely qualified. "The angel of the LORD appeared to him in flames of fire from within a bush.

Moses saw that though the bush was on fire it did not burn up. So Moses thought, 'I will go over and see this strange sight—why the bush does not burn up.' When the LORD saw that he had gone over to look, God called to him from within the bush, 'Moses! Moses!' And Moses said, 'Here I am.' "[14]

The voice identified itself: "I am the God of your father, the God of Abraham, the God of Isaac and the God of Jacob" (Exodus 3:6). Then God revealed to Moses his divinely intended life's purpose—to free his people from Egyptian bondage—to be the deliverer of his people that Moses had long since given up on being.

Knowing that he had blown it, Moses may have thrown in the towel on his life and his dreams. Perhaps he had given in to the belief that he was destined to be nothing more than a shepherd in a remote desert for the rest of his life. He may have been convinced that God wouldn't want to help or have anything to do with anyone who had blundered so badly.

But God loves us so much that even after we've blown it, even after we've done the unthinkable, he seeks us out. God reached out to Moses, sending him a much-needed message: that the almighty God still loved him and that there was nothing—absolutely nothing—that Moses could do to alter the way God felt about him. God was saying to Moses, "I love you unequivocally, and that will never change, no matter how badly you've blown it."

God sends that same message of love to all of us, every day of our lives, and we need to embrace this message if our lives are to turn around after we've blown it. The words of the prophet Jeremiah sum it up best: "The LORD has appeared of old to me, saying: 'Yes, I have loved you with an everlasting love; therefore with lovingkindness I have drawn you. Again I will build you, and you shall be rebuilt.' "[15]

Just as any good shepherd seeks out his sheep when they are lost, God seeks out us when we've blown it and are lost. But God also

sent another message to Moses. By reaching out to and seeking after Moses, God let Moses know that he still had a divine plan for
Moses' life. And God sends that message to us as well. Too often we
fall prey to the lie that our mistakes nullify God's plan for us.

Like Moses, most of us tend to believe that once we've blown it,
we'll never get another opportunity to do or become anything significant again—that our dreams are as good as dead. So we give up
on life and lose all hope until we discover that no matter what, God
still has a life plan for each of us—plans ordained for us while we
were still in our mothers' wombs, plans divinely woven into our
DNA, the very reason why God put us here on earth. And nothing
can destroy them. We have other kinds of dreams, of course—
dreams that are nothing more than echoes of daily events in our
lives or dreams that are inspired by our fleeting desires. But that
indestructible life-dream within each of us—the dream that points
us in the direction of our destiny—is of a very different sort.

Any of us can (and often do) blow it. We get lost along the way,
and when we do, we worry that we've wrecked God's dream for
our lives. But that dream can never be destroyed; it will never fade
away. It will outlive failure and disappointment and unexpected
turns in life; it can't be killed. God's plan for Moses, for instance,
was for him to be a deliverer of his people. That was what was woven into Moses' DNA. For that purpose he was miraculously rescued in infancy by Pharaoh's daughter and set on a path that seemed
to lead to becoming the next pharaoh himself. It may have seemed
that Moses was moments away from taking his God-ordained place.
He had come of age (forty), and his grandfather, the current pharaoh, was getting old. It seemed just a matter of a little more time.

But then Moses blew it big time by murdering a man, seemingly
destroying both the plan and the dream that was in his heart. He
fled into the desert and spent forty years believing that his life-
dream was dead.

Sometime during those forty years in the desert, his grandfather died and another pharaoh took his place. If only Moses had waited patiently and not blown it, perhaps he would have been able to free God's people sooner than he did.

But even though Moses made serious mistakes and time was lost, the indestructible life-dream that was his destiny remained. You see, God knows that since we're all chronically human, we're likely to blow it. Even before we start out on our life paths, I believe God has a repertoire of alternate paths ready just in case. His Word tells us: " 'I know the plans I have for you,' declares the LORD, 'plans to prosper you and not to harm you, plans to give you hope and a future.' "[16] So even though our mistakes may have surprised us and disrupted the current plans God has for our lives, we need to remember that what happened didn't surprise God. He has contingency plans ready to get us back on course. He is able to work all things together for our good if we love him and are called according to his purpose.[17] Our mistakes won't irreparably damage our lives unless we let them.

A wonderful illustration of this can be seen in the history of Persian rug weaving. Persian rugs are made with beautiful, intricate patterns that take many months, even years, to create. Thus the rugs are enormously expensive, and collectors pay considerable amounts for the finest handwoven pieces. As the popularity of the rugs rose in the West in the late 1800s, inferior rug makers in Persia started using a flamboyant but weaker knot called a Jufti knot. This degraded the quality and durability of the carpet but allowed a rug to be made in half the time. Gullible patrons purchased these second-rate rugs, believing they were getting masterworks. Rug experts bemoaned the practice. But in the 1920s, a master artisan named Emoghli began producing exquisite rugs that raised the Jufti knot to a new level of desirability. The very thing that most artists saw as a flaw and a symbol of poor quality, he turned into something of beauty. From what others rejected, he created masterpieces.[18]

Like a master craftsman, God is prepared to take our flaws, our mistakes, and weave them all into a new plan—a plan that will bring about the dream he has instilled in us. No matter what happens—even after we've blown it—God can turn our lives around.

4

REGAINING CONFIDENCE
WHEN NO ONE BELIEVES
IN YOU

When I was just twelve years old, I had a baseball coach whom I called Mr. C. His last name was too hard for me to pronounce, and I don't remember it now; but I do remember how encouraging Mr. C was to me. Every time I pitched, he would stand next to me in pregame warm-ups and say things like, "Who's going to be able to hit that pitch?" or "Wow, I couldn't even see that pitch, it was so fast," or "I couldn't even hit that." Then, as I was actually pitching in the games, he would yell from the dugout as I got two strikes on the batter, "Show him your mojo." That meant "throw him your curveball." When I did, I'd strike the batter out and be rewarded by Mr. C's cheers of exultation. I always knew he was proud of me.

Later, though, when I moved to another state and went on to pitch high-school baseball, Mr. C was no longer by my side. I had a hard time adjusting to the new pitching distance, which was an additional fifteen feet, so my control was not as sharp during my freshman year. I often saw frustrated looks on my coach's face if I walked a batter or fell behind in the count. That really bothered me. So to get over the hump, I often replayed in my mind the words of Mr. C—"Who's going to hit that?" or "Show him your mojo" and tried to relive those moments when I knew I had someone right there who believed in my pitching ability. It was never quite the same, but I have no doubt that Mr. C's encouragement and faith in me had a profoundly positive and permanent effect on me. Knowing he believed in me made me believe in myself and brought out the best in me.

Why Belief Matters

Belief is powerful. The Bible tells us that "all things are possible to him who believes"[1] and that "whatever you ask for in prayer, believe that you have received it, and it will be yours."[2] On a purely personal or social level, we all know how important it is for us to feel that others believe in us and how dependent we are on the belief others have in us. To be well-adjusted and successful, children need to know that their parents believe in them. Students need to know that their teachers believe in them in order to do well academically. Athletes need to know that their coaches believe in them in order to perform at their best, and employees need to know that their supervisors or bosses believe in them in order to do their best work and enjoy their jobs. That's just the way we chronically human people are wired. We need to know that others believe in us.

The movie *Hoosiers* is a compelling story about the power of belief. In the film, Gene Hackman portrays the fictional Norman Dale, a basketball coach who arrives in the small Indiana town of Hickory in 1951 to take over the school's beloved basketball team— the Hickory Huskers. He shakes things up, reducing the team to only seven players, including the equipment manager, Ollie, who warns the coach that he doesn't play because, in his own words, he's "too short and not no good." But Coach Dale is a man who practices belief. With steady discipline and encouragement, he forges the boys into a team, teaching them to work together to outthink their opponents. Soon the small team starts winning, moving up the ranks toward the state championship tournament.

In the regional semifinal, however, disaster strikes. Up by three, with less than a minute left in the game, one of the Huskers fouls out. Another boy has been sidelined by an injury. The only possible substitute is Ollie.

Coach Dale orders him into the game: "Ollie, we need you." But Ollie is riveted in place, staring at the floor between his feet in terror at the thought of going in.

The coach looks his reluctant player in the eye and repeats, gently but firmly, "Ollie, we need you now."

Ollie swallows, hurriedly removes his warm-ups, and enters the court. Around him the crowd begins to hoot—they can tell with one look that this five-foot-three player is no basketball standout. And Ollie's first few minutes reinforce their assessment. Given the ball, he promptly dribbles it off his foot and into the hands of the opposing team. They score, reducing the Huskers' lead to one.

Ollie gets the ball again and is fouled. As the opposing team's fans yell and wave their arms to distract him, Ollie lobs a feeble granny shot at the basket. The ball doesn't even reach the rim. Poor Ollie can only look on mournfully as an opposing player grabs the rebound and takes it down the court, sinking his shot for the lead.

Precious little time is left in the game. When Ollie catches a pass, the opposing coach signals his team to foul the hapless player. But Ollie manages to try for a shot—and though he misses, he sets up a two-point attempt. For Hickory to win, Ollie has to make both shots.

The opposing team burns a time-out, and Coach Dale gathers his team. Ollie's face is ashen, but he doesn't hear criticism from his coach. He hears just the opposite. "After Ollie makes his second shot—" Coach Dale starts, then locks his gaze with Ollie's, "and you will make that shot—get back on defense right away. There may be just enough time for them to throw in a desperation toss."

No grand strategy. No belittling comments. No desperation rebound plans. Coach Dale not only expects Ollie to tie the game; he expects him to win it.

The opposing team wasn't giving up, of course, just as our opposition in life doesn't relent. "I didn't know they grew them so small down on the farm," a player sneers, knocking Ollie's shoulder as the boy lines up for the first shot.

But belief is contagious. Taking a cue from the coach, a Huskers teammate encourages Ollie: "Don't you worry about that, okay? You just concentrate on what you're doing and put 'em in the hole. You can do it. Let's go."

That's pretty good advice for living, isn't it? Don't listen to the enemy. Focus on what your Coach has told you to do. Trust in his confidence in your ability to do what he expects. And then go do it.

The voices of the crowd crescendo. Ollie hears the catcalls, but he also hears his name being chanted. One shot in. The crowd goes wild—Ollie has tied the game. He lines up for the crucial second shot: it bounces on the rim . . . and drops through the net! The game is over; the Huskers win. As his teammates lift Ollie to their shoulders, the face of the equipment manager who was "not no good" radiates with the power of belief.[3]

When someone believes in us, it's easier to believe in ourselves. Suddenly, things that felt impossible seem possible. Belief is a powerful motivator. But the opposite is also true. If we sense that no one believes in us, our lives can begin a downward spiral that becomes almost uncontrollable. When no one believes in us, we feel as if we don't measure up. We feel like the kid who gets picked last on the playground or the high-school senior who doesn't get asked to the prom; and when we feel that way about ourselves, we stop moving forward along life's highway.

Remember my old coach, Mr. C? Things fell apart when I started pitching in high school and Mr. C wasn't there. Because I had difficulty adjusting to throwing from a pitcher's mound that was sixty feet, six inches, from the plate instead of forty-six feet, my pitches were often wild. I would walk five, six, seven guys in a game. For-tunately, I threw hard enough that no one was able to hit the ball—so at least I gave away walks instead of hits.

At the time, the movie *Major League* was popular. Charlie Sheen played a pitcher who was so erratic that he'd earned the nickname Wild Thing. It wasn't long before that moniker was given to me—and I started to believe it. I'd go out to the mound, and Wild Thing would echo in my mind. No matter how hard I tried not to be wild, I'd always end up walking a bunch of guys. I knew I had to throw strikes—the most important thing for a pitcher is to throw a strike on the first pitch. But almost every first pitch I threw missed the strike zone. I was always falling behind in the count. And Wild Thing kept playing over and over in my head.

After high school, I discovered that I'd been pitching my junior and senior year with a torn rotator cuff and didn't even know it. I'd had pain but had no idea what was causing it. And because I be-lieved I was Wild Thing, I didn't think to ask anyone about the pain. It never occurred to either me or my coach that my continued wild pitches might have had a physical—and fixable—cause: that the pain might have had something to do with it. Everyone be-lieved I was just wild, and I did too. I'm not suggesting I would have been a great pitcher, but if I had simply stopped to look past the as-sumption that I was wild just because I was wild, I might have got-ten treatment and improved my game. I was never able to reach my potential as a pitcher because, in my head, I was held prisoner by my belief that I was wild.

The power of belief cuts two ways. What do we do when the crowd's chants of "Wild Thing" drown out the cheers of the Mr. Cs in our lives? What do we do when everyone seems to think we're "not no good"? It's easy to fall victim to the negative attitudes of others. But we can take comfort in the knowledge that even when no one believes in us, God does believe in us and can turn our lives around.

The Bible provides us with an impressive illustration of that truth through a man whose life story is given more space in the Old Testament than is devoted to any other figure (not to mention more than fifty verses in the New Testament), making him a central character in Bible history. Over the course of his lifetime, he was a shepherd, a musician, a warrior, a general, a conqueror, a ruler, and a prophet. God himself called him "a man after his own heart."[4]

The great man I've described is David, whose impact and legacy were so powerful that people both in biblical times and today refer to Jesus as "the Son of David." Aside from Jesus, David is also the last person mentioned by name in Scripture, when, in Revelation 22:16, Jesus said: "I am the Root and the Offspring of David, and the bright Morning Star."

Seeing Potential

David didn't begin his life journey with that sort of exalted reputation but rather as the youngest of eight sons in a culture where birth order mattered and families pinned their hopes and aspirations on the oldest son. Jewish law mandated that at least a double portion of the family inheritance would go to the oldest son, and younger sons were to be subservient to their older brothers. At the tail end of a long line of brothers, and smaller than the rest (the Hebrew word for *youngest* in 1 Samuel 16:11 also means "smallest"), the one who watched the family's sheep while his older brothers went to war, it's likely that no one expected greatness from David. Even the prophet Samuel's initial response to the appearance of David's tall oldest brother, Eliab,[5] emphasizes how pervasive was the expectation that physical size, power, and position correlated with ability and the potential for greatness. People might have believed Eliab could be great, but David? Not likely.

But God saw more than others did. More than David's height or position in the family, God saw David's potential. God turned his life around, giving him a direction and a new life that no one would have predicted. The story of that turnaround began when God, unhappy with Saul as the king of Israel, spoke to the prophet Samuel, telling him to go to the house of Jesse in Bethlehem and anoint a new king.[6] (This was certainly an interesting command, as Saul was still king and had more than one son in line for the throne.)

When Samuel told Jesse about his mission, Jesse quickly produced seven of his sons. Samuel rejected each one of them in turn, though, asking Jesse, "Is there no one else?"

Jesse's response was something like, "Well yes, I do have one more son, but he's just a shepherd, currently out tending the sheep."[7]

One may think of shepherds as romantic figures surrounded by bleating sheep against a hillside setting at twilight. Shepherding, though, is hard work—it requires long periods away from home, guiding the sheep from grazing site to grazing site. You have to be on constant guard against wild animals, day and night. If a sheep is lost, you have to go get it and carry it back to the flock. On top of all that, sheep stink—which means the shepherd stinks. In short, shepherding was the sort of job one assigned to the bottom of the family barrel, or even just to a servant. That was the job David was stuck with.

No wonder Jesse and his family didn't think David was worthy to be part of the lineup of possible candidates to be the new king. He was the one they sent away from home with the nasty, stupid, smelly sheep. The family certainly didn't think of him as king material—you don't stick your best and brightest out with the sheep. David was merely the last boy of many, heir to almost nothing, useful for servants' work and that's about it. We might go so far as to say that no one believed in him, not even his family!

We aren't told how David felt about being overlooked, but we can guess. He was chronically human like the rest of us, so we can imagine how he must have felt deep down, even if he didn't say anything. Imagine how you'd feel if you were David. You've just walked in to see your father and your six older brothers all dressed up and campaigning to be king. Wouldn't you think, *Oh, I see. They're all dressed up, and I'm not. I must have been called as an afterthought. You didn't think of me to begin with, Dad. I guess I really am the consolation prize. Is that ever going to change? Am I always going to be an afterthought?* Wouldn't you feel that there had to be something wrong with you, that you could never measure up to higher expectations, and that you were destined never to be anything more than just a shepherd boy?

But when David appeared, God spoke to Samuel, telling him, " 'Rise and anoint him; he is the one.' So Samuel took the horn of oil and anointed him in the presence of his brothers, and from that day on the Spirit of the LORD came upon David in power."[8]

You see, God believes in us even if others don't, and causing us to know that he believes in us is the first step God takes in turning our lives around when no one else believes in us.

Imagine you were David in this moment. What kind of change in attitude would come over you? Wouldn't you think, *If God believes in me, I must be valuable, I must have potential, I must be special; so I should begin believing in myself*? Perhaps David felt something like that. Suddenly he wasn't just the youngest brother stuck out in the fields. Suddenly he wasn't someone to be overlooked. Whatever change in attitude David underwent, he knew for certain that God believed in him—that God saw him as no one else did. Where others saw an ordinary shepherd boy, God saw a king.

A famous story from the world of art echoes the character of God, who knows our potential better than anyone. In the early Renaissance, every city in Italy competed to demonstrate its wealth and power by commissioning grand works of art. The city of Florence was no exception, and in 1463 the board of works of the Florence cathedral commissioned the sculptor Agostino di Duccio to carve a giant statue for their magnificent church.

Di Duccio selected a nineteen-foot slab of white marble from the famed quarry at Carraro. But disaster struck—whether because the slab was too thin or the sculptor or his assistants mishandled it, the marble cracked. When the cathedral board refused to replace the stone, di Duccio denounced it as unusable and abandoned the project. Thirteen years later, the city fathers persuaded the acclaimed sculptor Antonio Rossellino to accept the work; but he, too, gave up the commission as impossible. The stone was too badly marred. For nearly thirty-eight years, what had been intended as a proud declaration of the city's prestige stood as a public embarrassment.

But in 1501 a young artist, a native of Florence who had been away earning his reputation, returned home seeking work. The city leaders saw an opportunity and offered the commission to the young man, provided he could use the broken slab. Fortunately for them, the artist was Michelangelo Buonarroti.

For the next three years, Michelangelo chiseled and polished the stone, laboring in a workshop near the cathedral. When he was finished, the city fathers looked at the work and decided it was too powerful to be tucked among the other statuary in the cathedral. Instead, the statue was set proudly before the Palazzo della Signoria—the heart of Florence's public power.

The sixteen-foot-tall statue depicts David just before the fight with Goliath—a unique departure from all earlier works, which showed David either triumphant or in the midst of the fight. The youth stands, his sling across his shoulder, gazing to the side as if watching his distant enemy, his expression a mixture of anticipation and uncertainty about the coming battle. Michelangelo had captured the crisis of faith—the moment when a person must decide to truly trust in God.

Today Michelangelo's *David* is one of the best known statues in the world, the subject of admiration by tourists and art lovers from around the globe. The broken stone that others had judged worthless was transformed into a masterpiece—all because a young man saw beauty where others saw only waste.[9]

Just as Michelangelo could see potential that eluded others in the discarded marble, so God believes in us because he sees differently than others do. That's what God told Samuel when speaking of another of Jesse's sons: "The LORD does not look at the things man looks at. Man looks at the outward appearance, but the LORD looks at the heart."[10] Like Michelangelo with the marble, God looks past our faults, failures, and shortcomings to the potential in every one of us. After all, who knows of our potential better than our Creator, who put it there! God believes in us even when others don't because he knows the potential within us.

God knows something that we also know intuitively: the potential of anything is related to its source. All of us attribute potential to what we perceive to be its source. We say things like, "He's smart, like his father" or "She has her mother's looks" or "He has the athletic ability that runs in his family." Although we are quick to point to fathers and mothers and families as the sources of obvious potential we see in others, we seldom remember what all of us were taught at one time or another: God created mankind in his own image and likeness and, since God's potential is limitless, so is ours—even though sometimes we and others may not readily see it. God does see it, of course, and that's why he believes in us even when others don't. God saw the potential in David when others didn't, and he sees great potential in us!

The Need for Passion

Although the teenage David must have been deeply moved by God's choice of him as a future king, there were still problems ahead. For one thing, the position was still occupied by Saul, and for another, David had probably never imagined that he could ever be anything more than just a shepherd boy. He surely had never, even in his wildest dreams, thought of himself as a possible king. And if we can't see ourselves as kings, we can never become kings. So as step two in the process of turning David's life around, I believe God engineered a plan to infuse in David a passion for being king.

Plagued by an evil spirit, King Saul commanded his servants to find an exceptional musician who could come to the palace and play for him to soothe him and rid him of the evil spirit.[11] According to God's plan, of course, the servants recommended David, to whom God (in anticipation) had given exceptional musical talent.[12]

Sure enough, when David played for Saul, the evil spirit would leave.[13] However, accomplishing that was not the divine reason for which David had been summoned to the palace. God had more in mind than soothing Saul. I believe God's plan was to create a passion in David's heart to become Israel's next king, a destiny David had not yet been able to envision. God's plan began to unfold.

When David arrived, Saul immediately loved him, even making him his armor-bearer, someone who would always be by his side.[14] That, of course, would position David in the palace, with an inside view of what being a king would entail. We can imagine how he must have felt, embraced by the comforts and surrounded by the riches and privileges of royal life. Perhaps his behind-the-scenes experience enabled him to see himself as a possible king—a goal he may have never even imagined before. It was a perfect opportunity for God to develop in David's heart a passion to be king.

Passion was extremely important—even essential—in David's turnaround. Imagine what his life was like before his experience at the palace. Would he ever have desired anything beyond being a simple shepherd? We've already seen that his family expected no more of him—they didn't even think to introduce him to Samuel until the prophet asked. Since no one seemed to believe in him, might not David have thought of himself as inferior and unworthy? He would have been no different from you or me. When no one believes in us, we tend to settle for less than what God intends for us. So God has to create a desire or passion in us so that we will want to become what he has created us to be. In other words, desire is essential if we are to achieve what God has in mind for us.

Desire, or passion, is an intense inward appetite for something—a hunger, craving, longing, or thirst that causes us to yearn for a particular goal or object. It is an urge within us that is so strong that it becomes a driving force, an all-consuming ambition that is unstoppable until we attain the coveted prize. It is an insatiable urge to stretch for something greater than we currently are. Rather than luck, it is desire that can move us from mediocrity to excellence. Desire is the force that separates spiritual achievers from spiritual drifters. In order to achieve a goal in life, we have to want it!

It was the impelling from just such a desire that led Trey Woods, who was born with only one hand, to defy what others believed to be insuperable limitations. Despite having a right arm that ends just below his elbow, Trey has never allowed himself to accept limitations. When asked once what he couldn't do, he had to think for a while before coming up with a reply: "I can't button the cuff on my left hand. . . . Oh, and I can't pole vault."[15] But he does everything else. In high school he was a star baseball player, a star track athlete, and junior-varsity basketball player until he set that sport aside to concentrate on his favorite—football.

Even though he was a phenomenal player, college coaches took one look at his stunted arm and passed, fearing limitations Trey knew he didn't have. So he decided to prove them wrong, trying out as a walk-on player for Sam Houston State University in 1992. The coaches were so impressed with his athleticism that they gave him a partial scholarship before school even started. In short order,

Trey established himself as a starting defensive back, becoming a star player and setting the school record for twelve blocked kicks, including eight punts, two field goals, and two point after attempts.[16]

But Trey Woods wasn't alone. Not long after he started at Sam Houston State, DaWuan Miller began his career as a Boise State University star cornerback—despite having no left hand. DaWuan's story almost parallels Trey's. He, too, was a star baseball player and basketball player in high school. The story is that the Boise State football coaches were convinced to sign him after seeing him scoop and dunk a loose ball when playing basketball in high school. It wasn't long before DaWuan was a standout for Boise State, snatching play-off game interceptions from stunned quarterbacks and their two-handed wide receivers![17]

On September 16, 1995, the Sam Houston State Bearkats met the Boise State Broncos on the gridiron—with their one-armed wonders starting for each team.[18] The score and the outcome of the game are listed in record books, destined to be forgotten. But the crowd will always remember the two young men who proved that nothing can stop the success of a person with a motivated heart.

As Trey and DaWuan demonstrate, when talented, motivated people apply themselves, they can accomplish incredible feats. We can all do amazing things with the special talents God has given us if we will only develop a passion and believe in ourselves.

If we don't have a desire for something, we simply won't strive for it. It doesn't matter how many times we're told that we should use our talent to pursue a goal or whether we believe pursuing it would be the right thing to do. If we don't have a passion for doing it, we simply won't do it. But armed with a desire, a real passion, we're unstoppable!

God knows that, so one of the ways he turns our lives around is by creating a desire in us. As Scripture promises, "Delight yourself in the Lord and he will give you [or plant in you] the desires of your hearts."[19]

When David was summoned to the palace, he probably thought he'd be going just to play his harp for the king. The thought of becoming king himself would have been far from his mind. Why would he have conceived of it? He wasn't a prince—he was just the youngest of eight sons, destined (as everyone around him would have assumed) to be nothing more than a shepherd. But God had other plans.

The Power of a Problem

After the passion to be king had been instilled in David, the problem of how to go about achieving that goal remained. Imagine the moment when the dream of becoming king actually awoke in David's heart. Wouldn't he have been just like us, glimpsing our dream but still oppressed by the feeling that no one believes in us? He must have thought, *But how?* He surely must have noticed that the reigning king, Saul, seemed securely entrenched. Even if something should happen to end Saul's reign, David must have wondered how a simple—even a musically talented—shepherd boy could ever hope to take over such a high position. It's at this point that God moved on to the third step in turning David's life around: presenting him with a problem.

David's father sent him to take food to his other sons,[20] who were with the Israelite army, preparing for a decisive battle with the Philistines, their archenemy. I'm sure David wondered how bringing soda and sandwiches to his brothers could advance his newly found passion to become king. But David persevered and dutifully took the supplies to his brothers.

Now the Philistines constantly tormented the Israelites by steal-

ing their crops at harvest time, and they were once again threaten-
ing to invade their land. The Philistines were a formidable foe: in
hand-to-hand combat, many Israelites would die.

When David arrived on the battlefield, he learned that the Philistines had proposed a man-to-man challenge: they would put
forth a champion, the Israelites would put forth a champion, and
whoever came out on top would decide the battle. The losing side
would become the other side's slaves. David also discovered that no
willing volunteer could be found among the Israelites. The reason
was obvious: the Philistines had chosen a literal giant of a man
named Goliath as their champion—a formidable opponent who
stood over nine feet tall, wielded a twenty-five-pound spear, and
effortlessly wore more than 125 pounds of armor. Fear had gripped
the hearts of all in the army of Israel, for Goliath was a seemingly
unsolvable problem.

There are three main kinds of problems: problems others cause,
problems we ourselves cause, and problems God puts in our way in
order to nudge us out of our present situation and put us on course
for the destiny he intends for us. When we encounter the third type
of problem, we have to stop, take notice, and get ready to have God
turn our lives around. Charles Swindoll wrote about problems as
"so-called 'impossibilities' " that, when brought into proper focus,
could be seen as God-given possibilities. He said, "We are all faced
with a series of great opportunities brilliantly disguised as impossible situations."[21]

God loves to turn our lives around by exposing us to a problem,
especially if no one believes in us, because when we solve such a
problem, three important things happen: people suddenly start to
believe in us; we reap significant rewards; and we begin to move
forward—and up! God knows that the ability to solve a problem
and turn it into an opportunity can change our lives and move us
forward. He knows that people who solve the greatest problems

receive the greatest rewards and are able to command the greatest influence.

We don't always see opportunities when life offers them to us. I'm reminded of something that happened involving a group of young musicians who eventually recorded such hits as "I Want to Hold Your Hand," "Can't Buy Me Love," "Let It Be," "Hey Jude," and "Strawberry Fields Forever"—tunes you may recognize as Beatles singles that went to the top of the charts.

Shocking as it may seem, though, when the Beatles were just starting out and auditioned for Decca Records, Decca turned them down.[22] I can't think of a better example of a missed opportunity. Maybe someone thought, *These guys are too different. I don't know how we can sell this music. Signing them would be a problem.* Can you imagine how the person who made that decision for Decca felt when the Beatles skyrocketed to fame under contract with a different label? I wonder how long he held his job after that.

The remarkable thing that happens when God puts problems in our way, though, is that he will do something to make us see those problems as opportunities if we will only pay attention.

And God did exactly that for David. Soon after David learned about the Philistine challenge, he also learned from camp gossip that King Saul would give great wealth to the man who killed Goliath and would exempt the slayer's family from taxes. The king would also give the hero one of his daughters in marriage.

I imagine that suddenly David began to see how he might become Israel's next king. Marrying the king's daughter would put him on course as a possible successor to the throne. So David, in whom God had already instilled a passion to be king, no longer saw Goliath as a giant-sized problem but rather as a giant-sized opportunity.

Thereafter, God advanced the turning of David's life around in two additional ways. The first was to show David how to make use of what he already had and to use the skills at which he was already practiced in order to accomplish his task. We've all heard it said that practice makes perfect. In David's life, that proved to be true:

> Saul gave David his own armor—a bronze helmet and a coat of mail. David put it on, strapped the sword over it, and took a step or two to see what it was like, for he had never worn such things before.
>
> "I can't go in these," he protested to Saul. "I'm not used to them." So David took them off again. He picked up five smooth stones from a stream and put them into his shepherd's bag. Then, armed only with his shepherd's staff and sling, he started across the valley to fight the Philistine.[23]

God had David use his sling against Goliath because that's what David had practiced with and was skillful at using.

A sling is no easy weapon to use. Unlike the slingshots we know today, made from a convenient Y-shaped stick and a strip of rubber, David's sling would have been a long strip of woven cord or leather with a small pouch in the middle. Grasping the ends of the cord, with a stone in the pouch, David would whirl it around rapidly, letting go of one end of the cord to send the stone flying like a bullet. But if he released the cord at the wrong instant, the stone could fly in almost any direction.

Using a sling took practice. So back when no one believed in David and he was out tending sheep, with nothing to do but stand there and watch the animals eat grass all day, he probably passed the time practicing with his sling. I can imagine the old clay jars he set up for target practice, aiming first from point-blank range and then from farther and farther away, until he had achieved deadly accuracy. Out in the meadows and on the hillside with his sheep, David became the Clint Eastwood of Bible times, the quickest draw in all Israel. Pretty soon the lions and bears learned to avoid the sheep watched over by this kid.

Yet even then, I'm sure David was a lot like you and me—questioning himself and thinking, *Look at me! The only thing I'm good at is using this sling! What good will that ever do me?* A sling was the weapon of peasants, not of royalty. Kings and princes fought with spears, swords, and bows and arrows. Nobodies threw rocks.[24] How could being an expert slinger possibly lead to becoming a king?

Most of us have experienced similar doubts about the significance or value of some talent or skill we have. You may recall the movie *The Karate Kid*, in which that sort of thing happened to the hero, young Daniel LaRusso, played by Ralph Macchio. Desperate to defend himself against school bullies, Daniel asks his elderly neighbor, Mr. Miyagi (played by Pat Morita), to teach him karate. Miyagi agrees on one condition: Daniel must submit totally to his instruction and never question his methods.

Mr. Miyagi sets the boy to work. First Daniel must wash and wax several weather-beaten cars using a precise motion with each hand: "wax on" with the right, "wax off" with the left. The next day Miyagi tells Daniel to sand his deck, using wide circles with each arm. Another day Daniel must paint the garden fence with up-and-down strokes. Finally, one day Daniel arrives at Miyagi's house to find a note instructing him to paint the house in side-to-side strokes. That evening, when Daniel is down to the last patch of house, Miyagi returns from a day of fishing.

His patience gone, Daniel demands to know when he will learn karate. The old man frowns. "You learn plenty," he says curtly.

"Oh sure!" Daniel yells. "I learned to wax your cars and sand your floor and paint your house!"

Miyagi commands the boy to demonstrate each of the motions from the chores, one by one. As Daniel does so, Miyagi throws punches and kicks. The motions from the chores block every attack. Without warning, Miyagi unleashes a flurry of blows, and Daniel instinctively intercepts every one, his muscles reflexively responding to the patterns they've followed for several days. The lesson complete, Miyagi bows to his pupil and leaves, leaving the boy to realize what the master has known all along: that even what seems mundane and insignificant can play a significant part in preparing us for our destinies.[25]

Just as Daniel had no inkling of the future value of the skills he was acquiring while doing his chores, David probably never dreamed that his skill with a sling would turn out to be a key factor in turning his life around—that his sling would prove to be not just a catapult for a stone but a catapult for his life, propelling him toward his God-intended destiny. But events proved that God had given him that ability for a purpose.

I don't know, of course, what it is that you're good at or what it is that you enjoy doing but may have undervalued, thinking that although it's fun, it could never be a factor in your success. I do know, however, that God can and does work all things together for good, even things as seemingly trivial as expertise in using a sling. So never count out a unique talent you have. It just may be the very thing God will use to bring about a turnaround in your life.

God finally completed David's turnaround by bringing a second tool into play. You see, even though David was practiced with a sling, he wasn't *that* good: God lent David his divine power. The Bible tells us that

> As Goliath moved closer to attack, David quickly ran out to meet him. Reaching into his shepherd's bag and taking out a stone, he hurled it with his sling and hit the Philistine in the forehead. The stone sank in, and Goliath stumbled and fell face down on the ground.
>
> So David triumphed over the Philistine with only a sling and a stone, for he had no sword. Then David ran over and pulled Goli-

ath's sword from its sheath. David used it to kill him and cut off his head.[26]

Although David was good with a sling, his triumph over Goliath was more a miracle than simply a feat of skill. Historians tell us that the only part of Goliath's body not protected was a little part of his forehead left uncovered by his helmet.[27] If David hadn't hit him exactly in that spot, and with the first stone, he wouldn't have triumphed over Goliath. God "caused" all things to work together for David's good, just as Romans 8:28 promises he will do for us.

David turned the problem with which God confronted him into an opportunity, and by defeating Goliath, he went from being a simple shepherd boy in whom no one believed to being a hero in whom everyone believed. His princely rewards from King Saul put him on the path toward his divinely ordained destiny as a king whose praises would literally be sung in the streets of Israel.

The wonderful news is that, in a similar way, God can do great things for us. He can turn our lives around when no one believes in us by letting us know that he believes in us, by creating a passion in us, by presenting us with opportunities neatly disguised as problems, by leading us to develop key talents (even if we overlook their importance), and ultimately by lending us his power.

5

FINDING YOUR WAY BACK
WHEN YOU'VE WALKED
AWAY FROM GOD

🐦

A man once told me he believed he had committed the "unpardonable sin." As a young man, he had given his life to Christ and then later walked away from him—not just being lured away by sin or thinking, *Someday I'll go back to God.* No, this young man had consciously chosen to believe that everything about Christianity was a farce—that Jesus wasn't really Lord. So he walked away, planning never to return.

But living life away from God changed his mind. He began to realize that he had made a mistake. The more he experienced life without God, the more he recognized how crucial God was to his life. He wanted to return, but he was afraid. Would God accept someone who had willfully walked away from him?

The man attended church week after week, but still he was overwhelmed by fear that it was too late; he'd gone too far.

Another man once came to me and announced that he had become an atheist. He claimed to have studied the matter scientifically and concluded that there was no God. So I engaged him on that point, asking him to provide me with the details. As we discussed them, he had to admit that every argument he had was flawed; yet he stuck to his decision. In the course of our conversation, it became obvious to me that his decision was not based on science or even on faith. Rather, he *wanted* his former faith to be false so he could pursue an adulterous relationship free of condemnation or guilt. If God didn't exist, the man could act without fear of divine judgment. His arguments weren't arguments at all; they were just excuses.

This man went on to pursue his new, "free" philosophy. But things didn't turn out as he imagined they would. Instead of freedom, his life spiraled down into great relational pain. As he struggles to pick up the pieces—still independent of God—when asked about coming back to Jesus, he simply replies: "If I ever did it, I see it taking a long time."

Jesus knew about both these men long before they made their decisions; he even told a story about someone not so different from them. It's the story of a boy who walked away from his loving father, made all sorts of ruinous mistakes, returned to his father to beg for forgiveness, and was welcomed back unhesitatingly—with love and without question.

As the story goes, the younger of a man's two sons went to his father one day and asked that he be given the portion of his father's possessions that was due him as his inheritance. The father obliged, and after a few days, the boy took what his father gave him and traveled to a distant country, where he wasted it all in profligate living. In desperation, he begged a local citizen of that country for a job, and the man sent him into the fields to feed his swine. With no one else willing to help him, and finding himself in a situation where his only sustenance might be the same slop he was feeding the pigs, the young man remembered that even his father's servants were better fed and cared for than that.

I'll return home, he thought, *and beg my father to forgive me. I'll confess my sins and failures and ask him to make me like one of his hired servants.* And so he set out to return to his father.

While he was still a distance away, his father saw him and compassionately ran to him, welcoming and embracing him. The boy began to beg for his father's forgiveness, confessing his sin and protesting that he was no longer worthy to be called his father's son. But the father, overjoyed to have his son back, interrupted the prepared speech and simply turned to his servants and said, "Quick! Bring the best robe and put it on him. Put a ring on his finger and sandals on his feet. Bring the fattened calf and kill it. Let's have a feast and celebrate. For this son of mine was dead and is alive again; he was lost and is found."[1]

That, of course, is the story of the prodigal son, and the father that the boy walked away from was his earthly father. But Jesus told the story because we can also be prodigal and walk away from our heavenly Father.

Why We Walk Away

Have you ever walked away from God? If you have, you know that you didn't just wake up one day and say to yourself, "I've decided to walk away from God. I've had it with all this Christianity stuff," or "I'm tired of following all those rules and watching all my p's and q's, so I'm going to stop trying to do things God's way and just do whatever I want to do my own way."

Despite the claims of the two men at the beginning of this chapter, walking away from God just doesn't happen that way. I'm convinced they both came to their decisions over time, maybe not even realizing all the little things that turned them aside. Walking away from God is a gradual process. Let's look at a number of possible reasons why it happens.

DISAPPOINTMENT WITH GOD

Things don't always turn out the way we hope or expect. When they don't, we often blame God. Perhaps we're disappointed because we didn't get the promotion we wanted and prayed for, or because our marriage isn't working out, or because financial help we need never comes through, or because a sick loved one for whom we've prayed doesn't get better. We ask for God's help, but he seems silent. He doesn't do things our way—so we reject him.

DISAPPOINTMENT WITH PEOPLE

We might withdraw into ourselves and turn our backs on God if we are hurt or offended by other people—for instance, when people we thought were our friends don't bother to visit us when we're sick . . . when they gossip about us, criticize our character, or are disloyal to us. We forget that, like us, other people are chronically human. Especially if these people claim to be followers of Jesus, we rush to assign their flaws and failings to God. We decide that since these people haven't shown us the grace we expect from God, it's somehow God's fault.

TEMPTATION

Our failure to avoid temptation can also be a factor in losing faith and walking away from God. When we're tempted, we may try to resist; but sometimes the temptation doesn't go away. Or it may seem to go away for a while, but before long, it's back with an even stronger pull. Again we may try to resist, but not so fiercely and with less determination. We may finally stop resisting and just give in, disappointed with ourselves but equally disappointed with God for seeming to ignore our problems and failing to help us. We even go so far as to make God a scapegoat, blaming him for problems we've caused ourselves.

Jesus' half brother James addressed that issue in the book of the Bible that bears his name: "When tempted, no one should say, 'God is tempting me.' For God cannot be tempted by evil, nor does he tempt anyone; but each one is tempted when, by his own evil de-sire, he is dragged away and enticed. Then, after desire has con-ceived, it gives birth to sin; and sin, when it is full-grown, gives birth to death."[2]

Walking away from God is a gradual process. James says we are dragged away from God by our desires, by the things or ideas that entice us. Enticement is subtle. It may seem innocent at first—just a glance, or a little wish, or a minor grumble that things aren't go-ing our way—but eventually it grows until we are trapped in obses-sion, selfishness, or bitterness. That's when we walk away—and we're the ones responsible.

As James points out, God is neither subject to temptation, nor does he tempt us. In other words, God is not responsible for evil. An atheist once told me that the reason he didn't believe in God was that if there really was a God and he was good, there wouldn't be so much evil in the world. So I challenged him: "All right, let's assume that God doesn't exist, as you seem to think. If God doesn't exist, where does all that evil come from?"

When he admitted that it would have to mean that man brings evil upon himself, I suggested to him that since we had decided that God isn't responsible for evil, we might consider bringing him back into the picture.

The essential point, of course, is that God isn't responsible for the disappointments, hurts, and temptations that pull us away from him. Walking away from God is a decision that we make ourselves. But it's the outcome of a gradual process rather than a sudden, un-expected, uncontrollable event.

ENVY

Let's look again at the story of the prodigal son. The gradual pro-cess of this young man's walking away probably began when he looked out from the safety of his father's house at how other people were living their lives. Maybe they were staying out late and partying, with no curfews imposed on them. Perhaps it seemed that they didn't have to put up with all the rules he had to live under. So he began thinking other people had it better than he did.

But one of the things we learn in life as we mature is that there is no more misleading myth than the one that tells us the grass is greener on the other side of the fence. As we mature, we come to realize that whether our grass is green or not depends entirely on how we care for it. If we take a person whose grass isn't green and move him to a new environment where the grass is green, in a short time the grass there will likely turn brown too.

The prodigal son did not have the maturity to see this error. He gazed out over the fence and believed that the grass was greener on the other side and that his father was holding him back. He decided he could do a better job managing his life without his father's help. He may have nursed that thought for a long time, gradually moving further and further away from his father until he finally took that fateful step.

How God Turns Our Lives Around

Even though we move away from our heavenly father, he loves us so much that he is still able and willing to turn our lives around. Jesus used the story of the prodigal son to illustrate that point, adding details that demonstrate the depth of God's love for us. But in order to truly grasp the deep love Jesus described, we need to understand the story as the people to whom it was originally told would have understood it. You see, Jesus knew his culture—he knew how people thought of fathers and sons and the ways they would and should behave. And as we come to understand what Jesus' listeners would have expected from the story—and what they heard instead—we, too, can learn what Jesus was teaching: that God is a Father like no other.

HE LETS US GO

The father in Jesus' story starts out as a classic patriarch. Maybe you're from a family like that: there's one man everyone knows is the "head of the family." He sets the standards the family lives by, and woe to the family member who breaks Papa's rules! He's in control, and everybody knows it. That's the sort of father Jesus' listeners were used to: the man who ran his family by Jewish law and custom, the man who had control. He told his sons what to do, and they did it. That's what Jesus' listeners expected of fathers— and what they expected of God. But Jesus showed them that God is a Father who is willing to let his children go.

He lets us go despite cultural norms and expectations.

I once heard Bill Hybels, senior pastor of Willow Creek Community Church, telling about what some men had told him their fathers would never do. I decided to try the same experiment, so I asked members of my staff to make a similar list. Some of their answers were: "My father would never curse." "My dad would never pass a person whose car had broken down on the road." And, "My dad would never wear socks shorter than midcalf length." The most unusual was, "My dad absolutely refused to wear shorts. We could be on a family vacation in Florida, and it would be a hundred degrees outside and humid, and Dad would still wear jeans."

Sometimes the things our fathers won't do are personal; sometimes they're practical. But some things our fathers won't do have to do with the culture we live in. All cultures have rules—some written, some just known—but everyone follows them. Coach

Paul "Bear" Bryant, the legendary football hero of the University of Alabama, was known for his signature houndstooth hat. But he wouldn't wear it when his team played in a domed stadium because he had been taught to remove his hat indoors. That rule has faded from American manners today, but there are plenty of others we follow, sometimes without being fully aware of them: the fork goes on the left, tip the waiter, stand for the national anthem, call your mother on Mother's Day. Most of these "rules" are mild, some are practical, and some make no sense at all, but still we do them. And even today, some rules are so ingrained in us that to break them is shocking, if not outright scandalous. For example, some Asian cultures consider dog meat a delicacy. But if you were to announce you had tasted "man's best friend" among a group of Americans, I guarantee you'd horrify many around you. The very thought goes against our cultural upbringing. It's just not done.

When we think about the prodigal son, it's easy for modern readers to overlook the severity of the boy's request. We think he was just greedy, selfish, and foolish; we don't think it unusual that a young man would want to sow some wild oats. He may have been slightly callous and ungrateful, but we don't see anything malicious in his request.

That's not the way Jesus' hearers would have thought. You see, in Middle Eastern culture (both in Jesus' time and today), no loving son, however selfish, would have made such a request. And no father would have honored it. A father of that day wouldn't have considered giving any portion of his estate to a son until, from the father's deathbed, the estate would be awarded in a ritual blessing that hearkens back to the time of Isaac—thousands of years before Christ.[3] Furthermore, there was no rightful expectation of an equal share. The eldest son was the primary heir; his amount of the estate would be double what any younger sons would receive, and with it would go the expectations of leadership and social rank.[4] The younger son's request wasn't merely selfish; it was grossly offensive, even scandalous. It just wasn't done.

In fact, it still isn't done. In his book *Poet and Peasant and Through Peasant Eyes*, Ken Bailey wrote:

> For over fifteen years I have been asking people of all walks of life from Morocco to India and from Turkey to Sudan about the implication of a son's request for his inheritance while the father is still living. The answer has almost always been emphatically the same. . . . The conversation runs as follows:
> "Has anyone ever made such a request in your village?"
> "Never!"
> "Could anyone ever make such a request?"
> "Impossible!"
> "If anyone ever did, what would happen?"
> "His father would beat him, of course!"
> "Why?"
> "This request means—he wants his father to die!"[5]

The people listening as Jesus told the story must have been sitting on the edges of their seats, thinking, *I know what's going to happen next. The father is going to beat the boy senseless! He's going to use the rod of education on his seat of understanding and set the boy straight.*

But that's not what happened. According to the story as Jesus told it, the father "divided to them his livelihood."[6]

So why did Jesus tell it that way? Well, the story is a parable—a story crafted for the purpose of making a point. The boy was past the point of reason, past the point of learning from his father's wisdom and instruction; so, in an act of absolute love, the father chose to let his son go. He chose not only to go against his firmly held cultural "rules," but also to suffer the terrible pain of having to let his son go his own way so that the boy might learn from his own mistakes.

That's the painful but loving way God often chooses to turn our lives around after we've walked away from him. He loves us enough to let us go so that we can learn from our mistakes when we won't learn any other way.

He lets us go physically and emotionally.

So what do we do when our children turn their backs on us? We do the only thing we can do: we let them go because we love them enough to let them learn from their own experiences, even if doing so is heartrending.

Letting go is never easy. But sometimes it's essential. In the late winter of 2005, one mother in New York was forced to let go of her son to save his life—literally. Tracinda Foxe and her infant son, little Eric Guzman, were trapped in a burning apartment on the third floor. As the fire raged, Tracinda took a desperate chance: crying out to people watching below, she held her one-month-old baby boy out of the window, breathed a prayer, and let go.

What a horrifying moment for a mother. Surrounded by flames, smoke billowing from her apartment, she did the only thing she knew to do: trust her son to God.

And God heard. Below, on the ground, watched Felix Vazquez, a catcher for a local amateur-league baseball team. He raced up to catch the baby as little Eric left his mother's arms. Firefighters arrived in time to rescue Tracinda, and mother and son were reunited, safe and sound.

"I said, 'God, please save my son,' " Tracinda told reporters later. "I prayed that someone would catch him and save his life."[7]

Can you imagine how hard it was for that mother to let go? She knew, though, that letting go was all that was left for her to do in an effort to save her child.

In my ministry, I often have the honor of counseling young couples before marriage. Most of the time, it is a great pleasure. But every once in a while, I run into a situation where I have grave doubts about the choice two people are making. One such incident several years ago stands out in my mind.

When I met with this couple, I quickly sensed that something was wrong. Though they both said they wanted the marriage, and both were adults, the man rubbed me the wrong way. He didn't seem to have his fiancée's best interests at heart. I knew her parents well and discovered that they shared my concerns. The young man did not show any interest in being a part of the family, despite the fact that his future bride and her parents were very close. They also sensed that he took their daughter for granted rather than treating her with respect. But being loving parents, they did not ask their daughter to give up on the young man; they simply suggested that the couple delay the decision. I thought this was wise and counseled the couple to wait and work together to gain the parents' blessing so that everyone could be happy and comfortable.

Unfortunately, the young man and woman did not listen to my advice or the concerns of her parents. In fact, they took the opposite approach. The bride moved out of her parents' home and in with the young man. There was no wedding.

Her parents were heartbroken but knew there was nothing they could do. They allowed their daughter to discover what life with the young man was like.

That life was as they had feared. Neither person was suited for the other, and both quickly became miserable. Within a few months they both realized it was a mistake, and she moved back home. Her parents welcomed her without condemnation.

As hard as it was for them to sit by and do nothing, the parents knew they had to let their daughter learn from her own mistakes.

He lets us go to learn from our mistakes.

Just as our children can turn their backs on us and give us no choice but to let them go, sometimes our hearts grow so cold toward God that he, in a love that is beyond our comprehension—and with a broken heart—lets us go, loving us enough to let us learn from our mistakes. In his wisdom, God knows that the pain we experience will soften our hearts and enable him to begin the next step in the turnaround process, which is to lead us back.

Remember what happened to the very confident prodigal son. After he had traveled to a distant land, he wasted everything his father had given him, nearly starved, discovered that no one would help him, and realized that he was in a seemingly hopeless situation. So he took the worst job any of Jesus' listeners could have imagined: feeding pigs, animals the Jews considered ritually unclean. Worse still, the young man was in such desperate straits that he longed to eat the pigs' food. He had hit bottom. His life couldn't be more off course. He was finally ready for a change.

HE DIRECTS OUR THOUGHTS

Look what happened next: "But when he came to himself, he said, 'How many of my father's hired servants have bread enough and to spare, and I perish with hunger! I will arise and go to my father.' "8

Did you notice that little adverbial clause, "But when he came to himself"? One version translates it, "When he realized what he was doing"; another says, "When he came to his senses." The implication in all three is that the son experienced a change in his thinking, and it came as a revelation. Nobody came by the pig sty and shouted, "Hey, dummy! Why don't you just go home?" No, he woke up. He had an idea. A thought popped into his head.

Have you ever had that happen to you—a thought just pops into your head? God often makes that happen to help us turn our lives around. I was recently watching an episode of *The Big Idea* in which a woman who had been fired from every job she ever had finally landed one at McDonald's—where she worked as a burger flipper and cashier. She hated the job.

But one day when she was at home, struggling to change the

dust ruffle on her bed, something happened that turned her life around. The mattress of her king-size bed was so heavy that she couldn't lift it by herself, so she called for help from her three children—all of them eight years old or younger. That didn't work either, though. The mattress kept falling on one of the kids. Then, as she was just about to give up altogether, a thought popped into her head: *Why don't I make a dust ruffle that zips on and off?* So that's what she did. Her idea not only solved her immediate problem, but—after marketing her product—also made her millions of dollars.

Another woman, whose husband owned a movie theater, loved to crochet. She would join her husband at work and sit in the darkened theater and try to crochet. Naturally, though, she had a hard time seeing what she was doing. Suddenly a thought popped into her head: *Why don't I make a crochet needle with a little light on it?* So that's what she did. Now she is making millions. Other ideas popped into her head too, and she went on to produce lighted scissors, lighted key chains, and other common tools with lights that people could use where a little extra illumination would help them. Thoughts that just seemed to pop into her head changed her life dramatically for the better.

Kyle MacDonald tells a similar thought-to-success story about himself in his book *One Red Paperclip*. Out of work and needing money, Kyle remembered a trading game he used to play growing up. He and his friends would start with one simple item and trade up to something better, seeing how far they could take it.

Kyle looked on his desk and found one red paper clip. He offered it in trade on the internet for whatever anyone wished to offer. From the paper clip, he went to a pen, from the pen to a doorknob, from the doorknob to a camping stove . . . on and on, trading up to something new and bigger each time. A year later, Kyle traded a part in a Hollywood movie for a house in Saskatchewan, Canada!

With a little imagination, Kyle turned one red paper clip into a home, a book, and even a movie deal.[9]

Have you ever had a thought pop into your mind that you just knew could be a solution to a problem many people struggle with? Have you ever had an idea that seemed so clever to you that you were amazed you could have thought of it? Have you ever had a thought pop into your head that you just knew would change your whole life if you could follow up on it?

That's God! God knows that thoughts acted upon have the power to shape our destinies. A nineteenth-century proverb says:

> *Sow a thought, and you reap an act;*
> *Sow an act, and you reap a habit;*
> *Sow a habit, and you reap a character;*
> *Sow a character, and you reap a destiny.*[10]

Indeed, thoughts can shape our destinies. God can send thoughts our way to move us forward if we're stuck, to move us up if we're down, and to turn us around if we're headed in the wrong direction. Just as the thought that popped into the prodigal son's head brought him back home and into his father's care, God can inspire our thoughts to bring us back to him even after we've walked away from him.

God turns our lives around by loving us enough to let us go and then gently speaking to our hearts to lead us back home. When great thoughts come into our minds, though, sometimes we have other thoughts too: *Can I really do it? Is this just my imagination playing tricks on me? Can I possibly make that happen?*

Like we so often do, the prodigal son began to have doubts: *If I go back home, will my father accept me? How will the people of the village treat me for disgracing my father and my family?* In that day and age, if a son had so publicly embarrassed his father—particularly a prominent man, as Jesus indicates this father was—the community would have gathered to ban the guilty party from village life; he would be shut off from all activity and conversation, unable to work or buy food.[11] And if his parents charged him with being rebellious or a drunkard, Jewish law called for the community to stone him![12]

Yet going home was the prodigal's only hope. It was either go home or starve. He had no other options.

I've come to be thankful for those situations in my life where God is my only hope. I'm thankful for the times when all other options have been taken off the table and I'm forced to do it God's way. I am chronically human, as we all are, so given a menu of options, I might not make the right choice: God's way. I believe that's why God, in his wisdom, sometimes takes other options off the table—to make it easier for us to come back home.

But comprehending the expansiveness of God's love can be difficult or even impossible, so we tend to devise our own plans for reconciliation. We find it hard to believe that God will accept us as we are or forgive us for what we've done, so we come up with a plan for acceptance that we can relate to. That's what the prodigal son did in response to the thought that God put into his head—to go back home to his father. He composed a speech: "I will arise and go to my father, and will say to him, 'Father, I have sinned against heaven and before you, and I am no longer worthy to be called your son. Make me like one of your hired servants.' "[13]

Note, however, that this went beyond the thought God had put into his head. God hadn't told him to go home and grovel. God hadn't told him to go home and do penance. God hadn't told him to go home and beg. God had simply told him to go home.

HE EXTENDS GRACE

All we have to do is ask God for forgiveness. God welcomes an opportunity to extend grace! He knows that we struggle trying to understand his thoughts. That's why the Bible tells us that God's thoughts are not our thoughts.[14] So after putting a thought in our minds to lead us back, he looks for an opportunity to extend grace. Grace is the third tool God uses to turn our lives around when we've walked away from him.

The prodigal son's father knew it was only a matter of time before his son would come back home. (Remember, in Jesus' story, the father represents God, whose wisdom and foreknowledge are as infinite as his love.) The father also knew that when the son came back home, he would be hurting and that people who are hurting and who feel guilty, ashamed, and embarrassed don't need a lecture or a heavy dose of extra guilt. They need grace.

The true nature of grace is what Jesus was teaching his audience through the parable of the prodigal son. To capture it fully, we have to go back to a couple of the things Middle Eastern fathers would never do: they would never divide up their property and give it to their sons early, and they would never run. Aristotle wrote, "Great men never run in public."[15] Running was for slaves. Running was for children. If something needed quick attention, you told a slave or a hired man to run to handle it—or perhaps one of your sons. Sons ran for fathers; fathers did not run for sons. It just wasn't done.

Yet Jesus stunned his listeners by having the father run—he not only abandoned his rightful seat of judgment within his home but ran through the village for all to see, running down the road to greet the lone, distant figure who by rights ought to have been banned from the community. The father ran, unconcerned that the village could see his aged legs beneath his robes, caring little for his lack of dignity—caring only for the ragged, dirty rebel coming toward him.

The people hearing Jesus' story knew all of this was scandalous: a son who asked for his inheritance and a father who ran. But they realized that the story was about our heavenly Father, who was (and is) like no other father. He is an amazing God who wants to pour out amazing grace on people who, like you and me, have turned their backs on him. The God of the universe is hopelessly in love with us chronically human people—so in love that at any point after we have walked away from him, he is waiting with a heart full of compassion and grace to welcome us home.

Notice a second point about grace in the parable: when the father greeted his son, the boy immediately began to recite his prepared speech about what he could do to earn his father's forgiveness. But the father didn't let him finish that speech, and suddenly the boy realized that the issue had never been about the inheritance. It was about his relationship with his father and about how he had nearly destroyed it. It was about his father's heart, which he had broken. So the boy at last understood that he couldn't earn his father's forgiveness. It wasn't his place to dictate terms or devise a plan, or even to think that he could provide compensation to repair whatever damage he had done. His homecoming and acceptance, if they were to happen at all, would have to be a gift of grace—a blessing that the son couldn't earn.

What is grace? Well, notice what the father in the parable did. He didn't just run to the son; he showered him with kisses and embraced him. That's important, because according to the customs of that day, if a son had disgraced his father and his family, he would have been banished or even killed. But his father ran to his son and embraced him, symbolically telling his neighbors, *"If you're going to banish my son, you're going to have to banish me too. If you're going to kill my son, you're going to have to kill me too."* By covering his son with his arms, he covered his son with his protection.

We Christians believe that this is what Christ did for us when he died on the cross. By his sacrifice of his own life, Jesus stood between us and the punishment we deserved to receive, blocking us from the blows that would have been ours. That's what grace is.

Grace is God absorbing our blows, blocking us from the punishment we deserve.

Grace is valuable beyond measure. If we have walked away from God, he will readily forgive our sins, accept us back, and shower our lives with underserved favor. God loves us enough to let us go, but he will send thoughts our way to lead us back, and he'll look for an opportunity to pour out his grace on us. But there's one more step God takes.

HE LETS US HAVE IT

Maybe you're thinking, *I knew it! There had to be a catch. I knew I'd have to pay. I knew God was out to get us.*

Not so fast. That's not what I said. I said he lets us have *it*. I didn't say *what*. What God lets us have is his goodness!

Notice what the father in the story does. He tells the servants: Bring out the best clothes from my closet and dress him. Give him a ring to show everyone that he's part of my family. Give him new sandals so everyone will know that he's not a slave but an honored son. And that calf I was saving for the big village feast? Kill it now and cook up the steaks. We're going to have that feast—we're gonna celebrate with everybody, because my son was dead but is alive again; he was lost but now is found![16]

The rebel returns, and Dad gives him presents and hosts a block party? Jesus' listeners would have been shocked. A Middle Eastern father simply wouldn't have done this! By Jewish law, the boy owed his father money for breaking up the family inheritance. The best he could hope for was to work as a servant long enough to pay it all back, which is just what the boy had planned. But even that much reconciliation would have been a stretch. As we saw earlier, as far as Jesus' listeners understood things, the boy deserved death. The son had disgraced his father. The audience might have accepted the idea that the son be allowed to work as a servant, thinking this strange rabbi was teaching them a lesson about retribution and taking your lumps. But Jesus went beyond anything they would have imagined: the father in his story was lifting the disobedient, rebellious youngster to a place of honor greater than any he had held before his disgraceful acts! That just wasn't how a Middle Eastern dad would respond to such a son.[17]

Maybe you can't believe this is how God would respond to you after you've walked away from him. But this is our God. This is the God of the Bible. He's so much different from the God of religion or the God the world has painted. Maybe you've been convinced that God was out to get you or that you were too unimportant or too pathetic or too undeserving or too whatever for God to love you. But that's not the way God sees things. He's not out to get you; he's out to bless you. He doesn't let you have it in anger; he lets you have it with goodness.

Why? Because God understands something that we and this world need to understand: there is a force more powerful than judgment or payback or getting even or giving people what they deserve. And that force is goodness—God's goodness.

The apostle Paul, who knew about God's redeeming grace better than anyone, said that "the goodness of God leads you to repentance."[18] Something happens on the inside of people when you let them have it with goodness. It's called a true heart change. It's called a turnaround.

Is it any wonder that, in Matthew 5, God tells us that if someone slaps us on one cheek, we should turn the other cheek to him also? That if someone asks for our coat, we should also give the shirt off our backs? If someone asks us to carry her burden one mile, we should carry it for two miles? Look at what Jesus is saying here: we should love not just our neighbor but also our enemy! He says we should bless those who curse us and speak bad about us![19] Why? Jesus tells us in the verses immediately following that list of unorthodox directives: "that you may be sons of your Father in heaven; for He makes His sun rise on the evil and on the good, and sends rain on the just and on the unjust."[20]

Did you see it? It plainly says that the reason we should respond to others with goodness—regardless of how they've treated us—is because that's what God does for all mankind. He's a good God, and he loves to do good—and he expects us to behave as he does.

One of my favorite scriptures describes what Jesus spent his time on earth doing—almost as if describing Jesus' favorite hobby. There's probably something in life you love to spend your time doing. Maybe it's fishing or golfing or playing sports or shopping or talking. Here's how the Bible says Jesus spent his time: "God anointed Jesus of Nazareth with the Holy Spirit and with power, who went about doing good and healing all who were oppressed by the devil, for God was with Him."[21]

I promise you, the God of the Bible, this extraordinary Father, is unlike any other father you've ever met or heard about. Even if you have walked away from him, he's ready to turn your life around. He's waiting and eager to run down the road, to run past anything the world says about you or you say about yourself, to sweep you up in his arms of grace, and to let you have all the goodness he has in store for you. All you have to do is come home.

6

TRUSTING GOD WHEN
LIFE'S OUT OF CONTROL

I recently scheduled a trip to Russia that would entail several long flights. The first leg of my journey was from New York to Kiev, Ukraine; the second, from Kiev to Moscow. On the way back, I would travel from Moscow to South Korea and from South Korea to Los Angeles, and then across the country to my home in Connecticut. I planned to spend some of those hours studying, but I also wanted to relax a little. So before I left, I downloaded several movies onto my iPod (proof that I'm a hip pastor).

One of the movies I downloaded was *Get Smart*. I was really looking forward to seeing that movie because, as a kid, I watched the original *Get Smart* television show all the time. I loved watching Don Adams as the bumbling secret agent Maxwell Smart, Agent 86 for the ultrasecret spy organization CONTROL. In nearly every episode, Smart would battle with CONTROL's evil counterpart, KAOS. While the obvious theme was that control was good and chaos was bad, a lot of the humor revolved around the fact that everything at CONTROL—particularly everything involving Maxwell Smart—was almost always out of control. Maxwell Smart tried to appear as the dapper, clever, and smooth superagent but invariably was more Bozo than Bond. He'd fumble his way through situation after situation, acting as if he were in control when he clearly wasn't. And the more control Maxwell Smart tried to have, the crazier things got. With Smart involved, CONTROL was more chaotic than KAOS.

As silly as the show was, it illustrates a great point. All of us want to have control in our lives. In fact, just like Maxwell Smart, we pretend we have it every day. We want to have control at work and at home. We tell ourselves, "If I could just get everything under control, it would be all right." Of course, what we mean is our personal control. But the truth is that very little of our lives is under our control. And like Agent 86, invariably, the more we try to control things, the more chaotic things get. Just as Maxwell Smart never really seems to "get smart" but keeps bumbling on in episode after episode, we do the same crazy, controlling things day after day.

Who's in Control

No matter how impossible it may be, we still want to be in control. Perhaps that's why the statement in Romans 8:28 is troubling to us—the one where "God causes everything to work together for the good of those who love God and are called according to his purpose for them" (NLT). It's troubling because we don't like it when the outcome of anything is dependent on someone or something other than ourselves. We would prefer to believe that *we* can cause all things to work together for our own good.

That's not what the verse says, though. It tells us that "God causes . . ." This grates against our almost universal desire for control. Quite a few of us even push our preoccupation with personal control to the point of becoming "control freaks." We may be close to that level of control mania, for example, if

- we think that other people's ideas are rarely better than ours.
- we think we're always or usually right about everything.

- we always take notes ourselves at meetings because we don't trust anyone else to do it right.
- we think (when eating with others at a restaurant) that it's sensible to order for everyone to save time.
- we think everything would fall apart if we should take a holiday from work and weren't personally on hand to manage things.
- before going on a vacation, we personally inspect everyone's suitcases to make sure they're properly packed.

I don't think of myself as a control freak, but I have to admit that when I'm not in control of a situation, I can become nervous and uncomfortable. Now, to be honest, there's really not all that much in life that I can control. I like to think there is, but in reality, there isn't. But the one thing I've decided I can control is my message on Sunday morning. I prepare in great detail. I go over my notes incessantly. I write the notes out—everything I'm going to say, down to the jokes—word for word. And then I rehearse over and over again until I memorize it all. That way, when I get up to speak, I know exactly what's coming, and I know exactly how to say it. I've planned where the inflections and emphases need to be, down to the tiniest detail. I'm in control, and that makes me comfortable.

But occasionally God steps in to shake things up. Sometimes when I go into a service, I suddenly feel God leading me to speak on a totally different subject than the one I've prepared. That scares the living daylights out of me, because I'm not in control of what's going to come next. I don't have notes to refer to, so I can't flip the page if I lose my place. I have to get up there to speak and rely 100 percent on God to give me the words. In those moments, everything is coming straight from God speaking to my heart. And I have to trust, not only that God is going to give me the words, but also that it's all going to make sense—that there's going to be some order to it.

When I speak, I like to have an introduction, a Bible story that drives the main point, and a conclusion that wraps it all up in a way that's orderly and easy to follow. So when God tells me to speak on something else and I don't have my nice, orderly introduction, main point, and conclusion all worked out, I feel very, very uncomfortable. The control freak in me freaks out.

I'll give you a recent example. In October 2008 I was in the middle of a sermon series called "Living to Die, Dying to Live." The message I prepared for one particular Sunday was, "If you had thirty days to live, what would you do?" But during that October, the economic crisis was reaching its pinnacle. People were scared. The news was all about the failing economy, about people losing their houses and losing their jobs—and I was going to give a message on what to do if you had thirty days to live. I knew the people in my church were already struggling with questions like, What am I going to do to save my job? How am I going to pay my electric bill? What if I lose my house? They were being hit with fear after fear after fear. I realized that the message I had so carefully prepared would end up discouraging more people than it would help.

God immediately spoke to my heart: *Today I want you to teach them how to respond in a crisis.* Without any notes, without any preparation, while we were in worship, God gave me four points. *Here's what I want you to teach them today,* he said. From those four points I preached an entire message. I hadn't prepared it. I hadn't thought it through. I hadn't rehearsed it. All I could do was rely on God to control what I said. I was scared the entire time—afraid that I would sound like I was just "shooting from the hip," which wouldn't help anyone.

But after the service, more people requested that message than any other message I had preached the entire year. Many people told me how much that message had encouraged and helped them. Instead of shooting from the hip, I was shooting from the Spirit, because I was listening to God and letting him take control.

Learning to Trust

Although there probably are a variety of reasons we resist giving up any control, one is that we tend not to trust others as much as we trust ourselves. When we're dealing with other people, it may be a good idea to be cautious about trusting others too quickly or completely, but we must guard against allowing our reticence to trust others to slip into our relationship with God. Our whole relationship with God is based on trust. To make it possible for God to intervene, especially when our lives are out of control, trust is a must. As Proverbs advises us, "Trust in the LORD with all your heart and lean not on your own understanding; in all your ways acknowledge him, and he will make your paths straight."[1]

John D. Rockefeller Sr. was a man who knew about control, particularly in the areas of business and money. He used his knack for control to build one of the largest corporate empires the world had ever seen. Through buying and selling and working hard to not only control his own business but to seize control of competitors, he became the first billionaire in an age when even millionaires were rare. For all his reputation as a ruthless baron of business, Rockefeller was nevertheless a devout Christian who believed strongly in the value of charity. From his earliest days as a poor clerk to his life as the wealthiest man in the world, Rockefeller donated a significant portion of his earnings to charitable causes, from churches to colleges to missions. But Rockefeller also tightly controlled his giving, painstakingly examining every request, scoping out where every penny would go. From an early age, he had been taught never to waste any money; and even as a man who seemed to have all the money in the world, he couldn't break from that need for control.

Rockefeller's wealth, however, attracted a flood of requests for charity, from large organizations down to individuals, and the billionaire became overwhelmed trying to sort through the requests as well as run his business. The strain began to take a heavy toll: by 1891 his health was so severely affected that he lost all his hair— including facial hair and most of his body hair—leaving him, at fifty-one, looking like a man in his seventies. He also began to suffer from digestive problems and possibly stress-related ulcers. On doctors' orders, he switched to a bland diet including milk and crackers.

Then Rockefeller decided to give up his insistence on absolute control. He contacted one of the men who had successfully lobbied him to endow the University of Chicago and whose advice he had come to trust. "I am in trouble," he told the man. "The pressure of these appeals for gifts has become too great for endurance. . . . [Yet I am] unable to give money away with any satisfaction until I have made the most careful inquiry as to the worthiness of the cause. . . . Either I must shift part of the burden, or stop giving entirely. And I cannot do the latter."

"Indeed you cannot, Mr. Rockefeller," his confidant replied.

On the spot the billionaire hired the young man to manage his charitable giving. Rockefeller gave up control, trusting the wisdom of this friend to discern the worthy causes from the swindlers and schemers. Together they would build one of the largest and most generous philanthropic organizations in the world, the Rockefeller Foundation, which continues to fund medical research, the sciences, art, education, and other charitable works that benefit millions of people across the world.

As for Rockefeller himself, he took another step in relinquishing control: he stopped working. On his physician's advice, for eight months Rockefeller stayed away from his business, spending his time riding his bicycle, helping the hands on his family farm, and enjoying a simple, relaxing life away from the cares and control that had dominated his thoughts for more than thirty years. When he finally did return to business, he did so with his health almost completely restored. Rockefeller had no doubts as to where his newfound health came from. On returning to work, he promptly pledged a million dollars to one of his favorite charities, declaring, "I make this gift as a thank offering to Almighty God for returning health [to me]." Four years later, he would retire completely from his office, content to yield control of his income as well as his giving to others. God had given the billionaire a new and better direction for his life.[2]

Rockefeller's debilitating illness was a clear example of how devastating things can happen to us in spite of—or sometimes even because of—our effort to exercise complete control over our lives. Things beyond our control just happen. Bosses fire us. Doctors tell us they can do nothing to help us. Spouses tell us they don't love us anymore. Children become addicted to drugs or join gangs. When anything like that happens, we are forced to choose: we can keep trying to control everything ourselves, trying to cause things to work together for our own good; or we can put our trust in God and yield control to him so that he can cause all things to work together for our good.

As Rockefeller learned, trusting God and yielding control to him is the better choice. When our lives are out of control, our only viable choice is to trust God to do what we can't do unaided; we have to trust God to cause all things to work together for our good because we love him and are called according to his purpose.

The Story of Esther: God Is in Control

No matter what your circumstances may be—no matter how out of control they may seem—nothing is merely coincidence. Esther's story drives that point home nicely. At first reading, it seems full of coincidences. In fact, it's the only book in the Bible not to even mention God, prayer, worship, or anything that seems even remotely spiritual. But read it again, and you'll see that God is everywhere in the book of Esther. He's orchestrating every coincidence, choreographing every act. God is in control, working behind the scenes for the good of Esther and God's people.

The series of remarkable "coincidences" and unlikely happenings are visible evidence of God's presence, power, and control. The circumstances of Esther's life—and of our own—are not coincidences. God is divinely working behind the scenes to turn our lives around and work for our good.

Esther was a young woman plagued by circumstances beyond her control from earliest childhood. Her father and mother died when she was young, and she had been adopted by her older cousin Mordecai. Esther and Mordecai were Jews living in Persia, the descendants of those taken from Jerusalem by Nebuchadnezzar. Although she had grown up in Persia, as a Jew, Esther was still very much a stranger in a foreign land where all were considered slaves of the king.

With no control over her own life, imagine the struggle Esther must have had trying to keep a positive outlook. She may have thought, *My life is never going to amount to anything. I'm a slave girl without parents. I'm insignificant—just a number. I have no real future.*

All of us feel something like that when circumstances are out of our control. We struggle with our thoughts, with trying to keep a positive outlook on life. Our only certain recourse is to tap into the power that comes from trusting God to cause all things to work together for our good—even the things that are out of our control.

When we feel uncertain because life feels out of control, Esther's story can encourage us to trust God. God's control and constant working for good can be seen in four "rights" he gave Esther at key points in her story. The good news is that, just as we can see God's involvement in Esther's life through these four "rights," we can also trace God's hand working in our own situations and trust they'll turn out all right.

What are these "rights" that show God is working?

1. THE RIGHT PLACE AND TIME

One of the first things we need to learn when our lives are out of control is that we can trust in God's supernatural ability to put us in the right place at the right time. God's power to do that can be seen behind an unexpected happening in the life of Wesley Autrey. After entering the New York City subway station in the first week of 2007, twenty-year-old film student Cameron Hollopeter suffered a seizure while waiting for a train. The young man stumbled down the platform and fell onto one of the tracks, directly in the path of an inbound train.

Fortunately, Autrey, a fifty-year-old construction worker who was standing on the platform with his two young daughters, noticed what was happening and realized that nobody else in the station was going to help. Placing himself in great danger, Autrey jumped down onto the tracks, grabbed hold of Hollopeter, and with only seconds to spare, rolled with the younger man into a drainage trough cut between two tracks. An instant later, the train cars thundered over both of them with only inches to spare. Amazingly, neither man was injured.[3]

In the days that followed, Autrey was rewarded handsomely for his bravery. Mayor Michael Bloomberg presented him with the city's highest award for civic achievement, calling him "a great man—a man who makes us all proud to be New Yorkers."[4] Autrey also received ten thousand dollars from Donald Trump, a trip to Disney World, a year's supply of MetroCards from the Metropolitan Transportation Authority, and a "hero" sandwich from his boss. He then went on to make appearances on the *Late Show with David Letterman* and the *Ellen DeGeneres Show*—all because he had been in the right place at the right time.[5]

Now, I'm sure that Autrey never imagined when he left for work that morning that he was going to end the day as a hero. In fact, if he had set out to save someone's life or become famous, it's unlikely he would have even been at the subway station that day. Had he pursued greatness, he probably would have missed it. That's the way it is with God. We seldom have to chase his plan. He has this amazing way of putting us directly in the place he wants us to be. Then, as we faithfully go about the daily business to which he has called us, we find we're in exactly the right spot for God to use us in a significant way—like he did with Wesley Autrey. God has the supernatural power to put us in the right place at the right time to give us the opportunity to make a difference and to be significant.

Esther learned about God's ability to make her small place exactly the right place to do something big. While Esther lived her life in obscurity, God was moving things into place in the highest halls of power. At just the right time, the trajectory of Esther's life would intersect with the powerful king of Persia—and the course of history would be changed. Esther would be exalted to an unimaginable position of power, and the lives of her people would be saved. How did God do this?

The Persian king, Xerxes, was a notoriously power-hungry control freak who loved to manage everything to his own advantage. One of the ways he did that was by throwing enormous parties, to which he invited all the power brokers in the land so he could impress everyone with his social prominence and vast influence. He spared no expense when it came to impressing his guests with exotic food and lavish entertainment to showcase his unparalleled wealth and power.

One day the king decided to throw one of his famous (or infamous) parties. He invited all his officials and the VIPs from the 127 provinces under his rule. And though Xerxes, as always, was out to impress people, the party likely had a grander purpose: it seemed likely that Xerxes planned to top it all off by announcing that he was going to invade Greece, placing even more of the ancient world under his control.[6] On this occasion the king was particularly anxious to show off his beautiful wife, Queen Vashti.

In the first chapter of the book of Esther, the Bible tells us what happened: "But when the attendants delivered the king's command, Queen Vashti refused to come. Then the king became furious and burned with anger."[7] Imagine the quandary in which this put Xerxes. He had been telling everyone how he was going to conquer those upstart Greeks, but his own wife wouldn't come when he commanded. The queen's refusal was a direct and public affront to his authority and his controlling nature: it made him furious. When the king consulted with his advisers, they counseled him that the situation had to be dealt with quickly and harshly to prevent a women's liberation movement from being unleashed on the kingdom. (One can imagine them worrying that their own wives would follow the queen's lead and tell them to "stuff it!")

So the king did as his wise men advised, issuing an edict deposing Vashti from her high status and announcing to the entire kingdom that he would give her position to someone else. All this worked together to set in motion an unexpected opening in a prominent place. No doubt Esther heard this bit of juicy court gossip, but little did she suspect the true implication of it—that God was using his supernatural power to open for her a position of significance, to give her a new direction and a new life beyond anything she had imagined for herself.

Just as with Esther, right now, outside your realm of knowing, God may be creating a place for you—an opening that will turn your life around. You may not be able to see it, and such an idea might never have crossed your mind; but you should have faith in God's supernatural placement. In God's kingdom there is no shortage of significant places. God has a place of significance for you, and you can trust him to put you in it.

Yet God was only beginning to work. Vashti was deposed, the king's honor was satisfied, and the king and his advisers began searching for a new queen by holding a beauty contest. Each of the 127 provinces selected its finest-looking women, and all of the chosen contestants were sent off for twelve months of beauty treatments to condition them so that by the time set for the contest, they would look their best.

Through God's supernatural intervention, Esther was selected to compete and won the king's special favor. "The king was attracted to Esther more than to any of the other women, and she won his favor and approval more than any of the other virgins. So he set a royal crown on her head and made her queen instead of Vashti. And the king gave a great banquet, Esther's banquet, for all his nobles and officials. He proclaimed a holiday throughout the provinces and distributed gifts with royal liberality."[8]

2. THE RIGHT QUALITIES

Esther's success hinged largely on one important "right" God had made sure she was born with. Esther had the right qualities to be chosen queen. First, she was gorgeous—by design. God used the beauty he had given her to make it possible for her to achieve significance once she was in the right place at the right time. Second, Esther was wise and listened to good advice. She won the favor of and sought out and followed the advice of the official in charge of the king's harem—a man who surely had the inside track on what would please the king.

Even if we find ourselves in the right place at the right time, we must have qualities that enable us to take advantage of the situation. One of the things we need to remember is that God makes us the way we are for a reason, building us just so, so that when the opportunity arises for us to move into a place of prominence, we have what it takes to make the move. But it's still up to us to develop those gifts, qualities, and talents as Esther did in the twelve months—and possibly her entire life—leading up to her momentous encounter with the king.

Whether it's your beauty, your brains, your talent—even your peculiarities—God gave you your special qualities to develop and hone because he knew that you would need them at the right place and at the right time to make a difference for him. So remember that you've got the goods! God put them in you while he was creating you. God saw what you were meant to be and made certain you would have the attributes you'd need to achieve your destiny and make a difference for him.

Take pride in the way God made you, just as King David took pride in the way God had made him: "Oh yes, you shaped me first inside, then out; you formed me in my mother's womb. I thank you, High God—you're breathtaking! Body and soul, I am marvelously made! I worship in adoration—what a creation! You know me inside and out, you know every bone in my body; you know exactly how I was made, bit by bit, how I was sculpted from nothing into something. Like an open book, you watched me grow from conception to birth; all the stages of my life were spread out before you, the days of my life all prepared before I'd even lived one day."[9]

Like David, you have all the right goods to turn your life around and live a life of significance because God gave you the right stuff. God uses what we've got!

Let's return to Esther, though. She had been elevated from being a slave girl whose life was going nowhere to being queen of the most powerful empire of her time. So she was certainly in a better place—but not yet in the ultimate place God intended for her.

Have you ever gone from a bad place to a good place? When I say "a bad place to a good place," you're probably thinking about your personal life circumstances changing for the better. Maybe you're thinking about a situation with less stress, where life is easier, maybe even comfortable. If God blesses you with that experience for a time, that's wonderful. Be thankful for it. But don't allow comfort to cause you to think that you've arrived. God is not interested in making us comfortable; God is interested in taking us to that "great place" where we can be used by him for his divine purpose.

Esther was in a good place, but not the great place God intended for her. She had been exalted from obscure slave girl to queen. That was certainly a better situation for Esther personally. She lived in a palace, she wore expensive clothes in the latest styles, she had money, she had servants, she had anything a girl could want. Esther could have rested on her laurels and said, "I've made it! I'm living the good life!" But that was not her *best* life; it wasn't her full, God-ordained life. God's idea for Esther was not to make her comfortable but to make her part of his divine plan. Only when she was fulfilling her role in that plan would Esther truly be in God's great place.

Yes, Esther's life as queen looked good on the outside, but it was shallow on the inside. In the end, she was really just a trophy wife—a symbol that Xerxes had the best of everything. In his eyes she wasn't a person, she was a possession. But God wanted Esther to have a life in which she could be used by him for his divine purpose—a life of true significance, where the gifts he had placed in her could shine to his glory. So let's look at what God did to elevate Esther to that place of significance, where her life could finally take on the purpose God intended for it.

3. THE RIGHT CRISIS

Some time after Esther became queen, King Xerxes promoted a man named Haman to be second in command in the kingdom, perhaps to run things so that Xerxes could enjoy his power and control without spending too much time on boring kingly duties. Haman, however, was not a trustworthy man. He was a schemer and plotter, full of himself and his ideas—as vain and controlling as Xerxes himself. As one might expect in such a situation, Haman's promotion went directly to his head, to the extent that when Mordecai, the cousin who had adopted Esther after her parents' death, refused to bow down to Haman as he did for the king, Haman became enraged.

Haman vowed to avenge himself not only on Mordecai but on all the Jewish people. So he went to Xerxes with a deceitful plot, telling the king that a certain people were disobedient and rebellious and must be destroyed for the safety of the empire. (Haman was careful not to mention the Jews by name, lest Xerxes realize his claims were false.) And then Haman tempted the king even further, promising that if he eliminated this threat, Haman would be able to loot the alleged rebels and add ten thousand talents of silver to the king's coffers—an amount roughly two-thirds of the king's annual tax income.[10] Faced with a vague threat to his control and the promise of more wealth, Xerxes signed an official edict giving Haman authority to put all Jews to death eleven months in the future. Mordecai and the other Jews were in imminent peril. A fearsome crisis was at hand. But God often uses a crisis as a catalyst to cause us to step out in a new direction to meet a new challenge.

Remember what we learned earlier—that God will expose us to problems in order to provoke us into action, as he did with David by exposing him to the problem of Goliath. Now God would prod Esther in a similar way to push her to act to accomplish what God intended for her to do. Remember, God will put us in the right place at the right time with the right qualities or skills to accomplish his great plan, but something must encourage or provoke us to do the right thing. God gives us direction, but we must choose to take it. We might always choose to run from the crisis to which God exposes us, but we must bear in mind that it is by courageously taking on the challenge and solving the problem that we attain significance. As we learned earlier, problems can be opportunities in disguise.

4. THE RIGHT COUNSEL

When Mordecai learned of the king's edict, he sent word to Esther, urging her to go into the king's presence and plead with him not to do such a thing to her people.

Frightened, Esther resisted Mordecai's suggestion. She responded: "All the king's officials and even the people in the provinces know that anyone who appears before the king in his inner court without being invited is doomed to die unless the king holds out his gold scepter. And the king has not called for me to come to him for thirty days."[11]

Mordecai's famous reply sums up the attitude we should have when we fear losing the place God has given us: "Do not think that because you are in the king's house you alone of all the Jews will escape. For if you remain silent at this time, relief and deliverance for the Jews will arise from another place, but you and your father's family will perish. And who knows but that you have come to royal position for such a time as this?"[12]

Notice the four steps God uses to place us: first, he creates an opening; next, he makes use of the talents or attributes he has given us; third, he exposes us to a problem; and fourth, he challenges us through trusted friends. Trusted friends are like God's GPS for our new direction. When a GPS device tells you to turn, you need to heed it, or you'll miss your destination. In the same way, when a trusted friend challenges you to follow God's direction, you need to listen.

When Mordecai told Esther that she might have come to her royal position "for such a time as this," he likely knew the doubts she may have had about herself. He might have explained things to her something like this: "I know that for much of your life, things have been out of your control and that you haven't been able to see how your life matters. For most of your life you have lived without a sense of significance. You even ask yourself why you were born, what your purpose in life might be, what your worth might be. You've wondered if your absence from this earth would even be noticed, and you've struggled with loneliness, sleeplessness, and anxiety.

"But, my dear Esther, now is your time! You must trust in God's supernatural placement, and to do so, you need to see your life's purpose through God's eyes. God has taken all the seemingly unrelated things that have happened in your life—painful things like the loss of your parents, the slavery, all the things that cause you to wonder—and has supernaturally put them together to place you in a position where you can make a difference. Your life has not been a sequence of mere unfortunate accidents. Your life has meaning and purpose, and you need to trust in God's supernatural placement and begin to see yourself as part of his master plan."

The Divine Shift

Let's focus on ourselves for a moment before resuming Esther's story. Are you in a place in your life now where you don't want to be? Are you doing something you'd rather not do? Do you have a job you hate, where you're asked to do things you feel are beneath you or are unrelated to where you want to go? Have you had a painful experience that has taken you away from where you were comfortable and forced you into a less comfortable situation? If any of those apply to you, your discomfort may be evidence of God's bringing about a divine shift in your life that will ultimately position you so that you can make the difference in this world that he created you to make.

Confession time: I hated college. I hated accounting, which was the subject in which I majored. I believed—in fact, I knew—that I was called to teach and inspire people to be everything God created them to be.

The day finally came when I was invited to be an assistant pastor at the church which I now serve as head pastor, and I took the job for a salary of only $400 a month—a salary so small that for five years I had to work three other jobs to support my family. In addition to being a pastor, I was a waiter, a mortgage broker, and a bookkeeper and tax adviser. I hated every minute of it. It didn't make sense to me. Having to work four jobs wasn't my idea of significance.

Then, through a series of divinely ordained events, the church at which I was serving as an assistant pastor found itself in urgent need of a new senior pastor. I accepted the position, never dreaming that position would develop into what it is today—senior pastor of a megachurch. I "just happened" to be in the right place at the right time. Now, looking back at all the divine shifts along the way, from places I didn't like to places I didn't understand, I can clearly see how they taught me skills and provided me with experiences that have prepared me to go about making the difference in this world that God created me to make. For example, my hated job as an accountant and my experience as a mortgage broker readied me to successfully manage a five-million-dollar budget. The dreaded time I spent as a waiter equipped me to serve people as a pastor, and working three extra jobs just to make ends meet gave me a personal awareness of and sympathy for the average person's struggle. Looking back now, I can see that all of those experiences contribute to my ability to make the difference God created me to make.

Remember who God is. God is the one who causes all things to work together for the good of those who love him and are called according to his purpose. Our part is to trust his divine placement. Where you are now may not be the place where God ultimately wants you to be, but I assure you that it is an intentional step in the direction of his divine placement for your life. When we trust in God's supernatural placement, he turns around our out-of-control lives.

Notice that there are two parts to that equation. In God's divine plan, both he and we have a vital part to play.

GOD'S PART OF THE EQUATION: FAVOR

When the divine shift occurs, God goes even beyond turning our lives around: he grants us his favor. Back to Esther's dilemma: Esther decided to heed Mordecai's advice and trust that God had directed her to that time and place for a purpose, accepting the idea that God had a significant plan for her life—to save her people from genocide. But her decision to go unbidden to the king to plead for mercy involved significant risk: it was punishable by death. So Esther was facing the sort of precarious, out-of-control situation that challenges our trust.

Remember, although Esther was married to the king, he hadn't called for her—she hadn't seen him—in thirty days. Perhaps, in his eyes, Esther's beauty had worn off. Perhaps he didn't regard her as fondly as he once did. What if she was now only an afterthought to him? Fear must have made it seem as if the odds were stacked against her and that the chances King Xerxes would hold out the golden scepter to her were slim. Esther knew that by going to the king uninvited, she might really tick off that control freak—he might turn on her the way he had turned on Vashti. Esther needed Xerxes' help to save her people; she needed God's help to save her own life.

She asked Mordecai to gather the Jews in Susa to fast for three days in anticipation of her bold and risky request. Esther and her maids would also fast, surely asking for God's favor.

Then, as the story in Esther chapter 5 tells us, "On the third day Esther put on her royal robes and stood in the inner court of the palace, in front of the king's hall. The king was sitting on his royal throne in the hall, facing the entrance. When he saw Queen Esther standing in the court, he was pleased with her and held out to her the gold scepter that was in his hand. So Esther approached and touched the tip of the scepter."[13] The golden scepter was a sign that Esther had gained the king's favor—and God's.

The king's response is an important detail for us to notice. You see, in life, when things are out of control, we need to trust in God's favor. We need to trust in God's ability to cause people who have the power to help us make things happen to look upon us with favor. We need to trust in God's ability to make people who may not even seem to like us come to regard us with favor. We can trust God's ability to help us foster a favorable relationship even with people who previously may not have given us the time of day. A supernatural something is out there, a force that's available to you and to me, that can make all the difference in our lives. That supernatural something is God's favor.

About three years ago, I was trying—without success—to find a publisher who would print a book I had written. One publisher finally signed me to a deal—if you want to call it that. The "deal" was that I had to put up about twenty thousand dollars of my own money as a provision of the contract they offered me.

When the contract was actually in front of me on my desk, I heard the voice of God saying, *Don't sign it! Trust in my favor! I have something better for you!* But, being chronically human and, therefore, flawed, I disobeyed God's voice and signed the contract, believing I had no other alternative. In short, I failed to trust in God's favor.

Just a few weeks after I'd signed the contract, and as the result of a series of divine events, the *New Yorker* magazine did an eight-page story about me and Faith Church in Milford, Connecticut, where I pastor. Publishing opportunities began to pour in. Only a short time after I had failed to trust in God's favor, several major publishing companies were bidding for the opportunity to publish my books—and to pay me for writing them! If only I had trusted in God's favor, I would have saved the twenty thousand dollars my doubt had cost me. Even after my momentary lapse of faith, God did for me what I couldn't do without his favor. And God wants to do that for you!

Favor means friendly or kind regards, goodwill, approval, liking, unfair partiality. It is to prefer, to help or assist, to do a kindness for, to endorse. To receive favor is to be regarded or treated favorably, to be provided with advantages, to be especially privileged.

We're favored when we are treated in wonderful ways to which we may not be entitled. God's favor is evident when people choose to help us just because they want to help us or when favorable events occur that surprise us, making us wonder how they could possibly have happened. We know that God favors us when his face shines on us even though we've done nothing to earn his bounty. The Bible says, "You, O LORD, will bless the righteous; with favor You will surround him as with a shield."[14] It tells us that "his favor lasts a lifetime,"[15] that "the LORD bestows favor and honor; no good thing does he withhold from those whose walk is blameless."[16] The Bible also says of the Lord, "You lavish your favor on all creatures."[17] And finally, it tells us that "now is the time of God's favor."[18]

All of us need God's favor at some point in our lives to help us turn things around, especially when our lives seem to be out of control. We can trust in God to grace us with his supernatural favor and turn our lives around so that, in time, we will be able to echo the words of the apostle Paul: "Whatever I am now, it is all because God poured out his special favor on me."[19]

Esther put her trust in God's favor, and this is what happened: "The king asked, 'What is it, Queen Esther? What is your request? Even up to half the kingdom, it will be given you.' "[20]

Those who witnessed that event must have been thinking or saying things like, "What did she do to deserve that response?" Or, "Why doesn't the king treat me that way? It isn't fair!"

But favor doesn't always have to be fair. It's much better than fair! We needn't be envious of the favor God bestows on others, because God lavishes his favor on all of us. We can expect favor in the little things—sales at stores, good parking spots, unexpected refunds; and we can expect favor in the bigger things too—promotions at work, nice treatment from someone with whom we've been at odds, the best week we've ever had in our marriages, or pay raises. We can even expect favor in truly amazing things, such as breakthroughs in aspects of our lives that may have seemed unlikely to change for the better, or dreams coming true that we may have thought were impossible.

OUR PART OF THE EQUATION: TRUST

As you probably know, Esther's story ends in an amazing twist of events. She succeeded in persuading the king to allow the Jews to defend themselves against any attackers roused by Haman's plot, and the Jewish people were not only spared but became revered in the land of Persia. Many non-Jews even became Jews because they saw that the Jewish people had won the king's favor. And all that happened because an orphaned slave girl who experienced things beyond her control decided to trust both in God's supernatural placement and in his supernatural favor.

God wants to use and bless us as he did Esther. All we have to do is trust him. After all, consider who God is! He made us—each of us. He thought of us and designed us and crafted us before we were even born: "Before I formed you in the womb I knew you,"[21] he says. What's more, he crafted this entire universe with us in mind. The ground we walk upon, the mountains that rise from the earth, the plains that stretch out vast and golden, the oceans that sing with an endless voice—all were made for us. The plants and animals that dazzle us with their beauty, that provide us with food and clothing—all were created by God as a gift to us.

Why? Because God needs us? Of course not. As Paul told the

Athenian philosophers, God "is not served by human hands, as if he needed anything."[22] Why would he? He is the Creator, the Ruler, the King of kings. Everything in existence was made by him, and nothing exists without him—he owns the universe!

So why does God care about us? Because he loves. And the object of his love is us. He loves us so much that he came down from his place of glory—he set aside his majesty and power—to become one of us, Immanuel, Jesus. He came to walk as we walk and live as we live: hungry, cold, tired, thirsty, rejected, despised, beaten, mocked, murdered. All because he loves us.

And then, to prove his love and power even more, he turned his own life around—he rose from the dead, the ultimate turnaround! He showed us that even death is not a one-way street—all because he loves us.

So if God—who made the universe, who designed us and knows us, who lived for us and died for us and rose again for us—if that incredible, awesome God loves us and promises to bless us, who or what is going to stop him? No one can. The universe can't. The government can't. Your neighbors can't. Your coworkers can't. Your boss can't. Your enemies can't. The people who doubt you can't. Not even death can stop God.

No matter what, no matter who, no matter where, no matter when—you can trust God.

You can trust him to believe in you when no one else does.

You can trust him to turn your life around.

You can trust him to give you a new direction.

You can trust him to give you the best life you could possibly have—the life he has planned for you.

And all you have to do is trust him.

7

FREEING YOURSELF WHEN
YOU FEEL TRAPPED

As anyone who knows me personally is aware, I was trapped for years in a struggle to lose weight. I repeatedly prayed, asking God for help—but to no avail. Over a period of fourteen years I watched my weight go from 190 to 262 pounds.

Then one day the Holy Spirit whispered something in my ear on the order of: *Take note of some of the obviously weight-problem-related things you have a habit of saying to your friends—things like "I love food," "I just love to eat," "I could eat a whole box of double-chocolate Oreo cookies at one sitting," "I love pasta so much I could eat it for breakfast," and "I think I must just be big boned."* All at once I could see that my mouth was a cause of my problem, and not just because it was the opening into which I was stuffing an excessive amount of food. My body was obeying my mouth! Of course I could have rationalized, drawing the conclusion that, since I was praying to lose weight and believed in the power of God's help, God's failure to answer my prayers meant that it was his will for me to be fat.

Have you ever done that—assumed that because God didn't take away some personal struggle you face, he wants you to "just be that way"? When we assume that what happens in our lives or in our society is an indication of what God wants, we're engaging in faulty reasoning. If that assumption were accurate, it would mean that

God wants abortion to be a common practice, that prayer should be prohibited in schools, that it's all right for a high percentage of marriages to end in divorce, or that lots of people should end up in hell. My point, of course, is that we can determine God's will only through his Word, not by assuming that what happens around us is an indication of what he wants. And just as God's Word reveals his will, so our words reveal our wills—and often predetermine our actions.

Have you ever felt trapped—for instance, in a dead-end job, an abusive relationship, a financial crisis, or a physical illness? If you have, then you need to know that God has provided you with a powerful tool to help you find your way out; and the tool is right under your nose. It's your mouth, or more specifically your words. But since it's frequently our mouths that get us into trouble in the first place, we might not readily think of them as the tool God can use to turn our lives around and set us in a new direction.

My problem wasn't that God wanted me to be fat. My problem was my mouth. It needed to have the words that came out of it brought into line with God's words. So about eight months ago, I began trying to get out of the trap I was in by changing what I said.

Our words have power in shaping our lives and in changing the world! On a personal level, our words can help mend what is broken. Just think of the power that words like *I forgive you, I'm sorry,* and *I was wrong* have in mending broken relationships.

God literally changed the world with his words, as we are told at the beginning of the book of Genesis: "In the beginning God created the heavens and the earth. Now the earth was formless and empty, darkness was over the surface of the deep, and the Spirit of God was hovering over the waters. And God said, 'Let there be light,' and there was light."[1]

Notice what God did to bring light to dispel earth's chaos and darkness: he spoke. He used his words to change his world. And

God challenges you and me to do the same thing—to use our words to change our world, especially when we feel trapped.

The eleventh chapter of Hebrews, the chapter called "The Hall of Faith," features a running lists of heroes, stretching from Abel to the prophets as examples of faith. As we are told: "Faith is the substance of things hoped for, the evidence of things not seen. For by it the elders obtained a good testimony. By faith we understand that the worlds were framed by the word of God, so that the things which are seen were not made of things which are visible."[2]

When most of us read that passage, we naturally assume that "worlds" being "framed by the word of God" is a reference to God's creation of the earth by speaking it into existence. Although we know from the opening verses of Genesis that God did just that, the passage from Hebrews isn't referring to the creation of Earth. The specific original Greek word *aiōn*, translated as "worlds" in this passage, doesn't actually signify Earth and the planets but rather suggests specific periods within the past history of mankind. It is the word from which we get our word *aeon*. Note also that although we readily think of "worlds" as meaning planets and even stars (which is why, in this passage, the phrase is often translated "the universe"), the ancient world had no such concepts. To them, the planets and stars were not worlds; they were just lights. So the writer of Hebrews was not referring to worlds as we think of them at all. Nor was he referring to creation as a whole, because then he would have used the word *kosmos*, or cosmos—the Greek word for "the universe." Instead, *aiōn* implies the concept of "ages"—the idea of the Ages of Man, a central concept of Greek thought, which everyone in that time would have understood immediately.[3] When we combine that fact with the meaning of the word *framed*, which means to "put in order,"[4] the passage really tells us that by faith we understand that the ages—the history of mankind—were fashioned by a word from God.

When a devastating flood was coming, Noah heard a word from

God, responded to that word, built an ark, saved the human race, and through his faith in God, changed his world.

When Abraham was nearly one hundred years old, he embraced God's promise that he would be the father of many nations, and because he took note of God's words, Abraham changed his world.

God told Moses that he would lead the Israelites out of Egypt, and because Moses believed and responded to God's words, he saved Israel and changed his world.

Time and time again the great heroes we learn about in the book of Hebrews changed the world by embracing God's words and responding to them, and they succeeded in the missions God set for them. How can you and I embrace God's words and change our world? One way we can do this is by speaking them—by saying exactly the same thing about ourselves and our destinies as God says. That's precisely what the writer of Hebrews challenges us to do: "Let us hold fast the profession of our faith without wavering."[5] The core of that statement's meaning lies in the word *profession*, an English rendering of the original Greek word *homologia*. *Homologia* is a compound of the word *homo*, which means "the same," and *logos*, which means "word"—or, literally, "the same word." It means to agree or acknowledge or affirm, that is, "to say the same word" as the person with whom you are agreeing. A person who professes faith in God is literally speaking in "the same words" as God speaks—and that includes what God has to say about the person. The great heroes in the Bible believed not only in what God said about himself but also in what God had to say about *them*. They all had to agree with God's word about their own lives—to "say the same words" about themselves as God said about them. We can follow their example through the practice of always saying the same things about ourselves and our circumstances that God says.

Doing just that is how the great biblical heroes came to experience God's power to turn their lives around in the direction of their divine destinies. For example, when he was ninety-nine years old, Abram embraced God's promise and started calling himself Abraham, because God told him he would be "a father of many nations,"[6] and his wife Sarah, because God said she would be "the mother of nations; kings of peoples will come from her."[7] It was only when this happened that, in spite of their advanced ages, Abraham and Sarah were able to conceive a child. When they began to say the same things God said to them and hold fast to their profession of faith, they changed their world.

By extension, I'm telling you that your words have the power to change your world. Your words can change your marriage. Your words can change your health. Your words can change your financial status. Your words can change your job performance. In short, your words can turn your life around when you're trapped. Your words can change your direction and give you a new life!

I learned through my struggle with weight loss that words are powerful and that I need to take them seriously. They have the power to trap us,[8] but they also have the awesome power to change our world—if we harness their power through SMART Talk rather than falling into DUMB Talk.

DUMB *Talk*

You see, there are two categories of talk that we can use when we're trapped, and both of them are powerful. The first kind is DUMB (as in Drudging Up Meaningless Babble) Talk. DUMB Talk is what we're guilty of when we use what Jesus referred to as "idle" words[9]—words that yield no godly return, words that are thoughtless and profitless, words that are worthless, words that are unrelated to faith.

DUMB Talk is anything that contradicts what God's Word promises us or what God says about us. When you make a mistake and say, "I'm just so stupid," that's DUMB Talk. You're not stupid; you just made a mistake. But when you blow up that mistake into a condemnation of the intelligence God gave you, that's DUMB Talk. Or let's say you struggle with something over and over, and you say, "I'm never going to get past this particular thing." That, too, is DUMB Talk. You've extended a problem of the moment into an eternal obstacle, denying God's ability to solve it.

DUMB Talk gets you to assume that a season of unfortunate events is inevitable because of who you are: "I'm sabotaged. I'm cursed. Bad things always happen to me. This is just my lot in life." DUMB Talk makes you think what your parents did must be what you'll do: "I'm doomed to repeat my mother's mistakes"; "I can't help but follow the same path as my father." All of that is DUMB Talk. And remember when I said all those things about my weight problems—"I just love food. I'm just one of those people who's meant to be fat"? I was using DUMB Talk too.

SMART Talk

Fortunately, God gives us a better alternative—SMART Talk—a positive and productive way of speaking that involves coordinating our speech with God's will and plan for our lives so that our words are like God's and, therefore, reflect what God wants for us.

So how do we practice SMART Talk? We can answer that question in steps corresponding to each of the letters in the word *SMART*.

SPEAK THE END FROM THE BEGINNING

Right from the onset of what we intend to do, we must begin declaring how the situation is going to end. Speak the end from the beginning. We must begin talking about our circumstances, our situation, our marriages, our children, our health, our finances, our jobs, ourselves, or whatever we want to control, in words that describe exactly the way we want things to end.

God is in the business of "declaring the end from the beginning,"[10] and throughout Scripture, God demonstrates this truth. Before Abraham was a father at all, God promised the Holy Land to Abraham's descendants.[11] And before Isaac was even conceived, God began to call Abraham "father of many nations."

Jesus spoke in the same way. Once, when he was told that a young girl he'd been asked to heal was already dead, Jesus rebuked the mourners: " 'Stop wailing,' Jesus said. 'She is not dead but asleep.' They laughed at him, knowing that she was dead. But he took her by the hand and said, 'My child, get up!' Her spirit returned, and at once she stood up."[12]

Throughout his ministry, Jesus repeated this pattern. When he was traveling to heal his friend Lazarus, he told his disciples, "Our friend Lazarus has fallen asleep; but I am going there to wake him up."[13] His disciples couldn't figure this out—why go all the way to Bethany to wake up a sleeping man? If Lazarus was able to sleep, certainly it meant he was getting better. Finally the Lord told them flat out (perhaps with an exasperated sigh), "Lazarus is dead, and for your sake I am glad I was not there, so that you may believe. But let us go to him."[14] In essence, Jesus was saying, "Come on, guys! Follow me on this! We're going to go raise Lazarus from the dead, so we're talking about the situation the way we want it to turn out. This is how faith works!"

As God declared to Isaiah, and as Jesus showed over and over, God speaks the end from the beginning. Furthermore, God invites us to imitate him,[15] to act as he acts. When we imitate God, we do so not only in our actions but in our words. When we speak as God does, we use our words to declare what the end of our situation is going to be, right from the beginning.

We can recall the story of David and Goliath again as an indication of what we can expect to happen when we declare the end from the beginning. If we were to be asked how David defeated Goliath, most of us might answer, "with a stone and a sling." But David set his victory in motion well before he took sling in hand and ran out to face Goliath. Listen to what he said to the giant with whom he was about to do combat:

> "You come to me with a sword, with a spear, and with a javelin. But I come to you in the name of the LORD of hosts, the God of the armies of Israel, whom you have defied. This day the LORD will deliver you into my hand, and I will strike you and take your head from you. And this day I will give the carcasses of the camp of the Philistines to the birds of the air and the wild beasts of the earth, that all the earth may know that there is a God in Israel. Then all this assembly shall know that the LORD does not save with sword and spear; for the battle is the LORD's, and He will give you into our hands."[16]

And so it was.

Did you get that? Even before the onset of the battle, David declared how it was going to end. David used his words—his SMART Talk—to free himself from the trap he was in so that God could turn his life around.

MAKE A MENTAL PICTURE OF WHAT GOD HAS PROMISED

When we're trapped and need to have God turn our lives around, we need to form a mental image of what he has promised. We must meditate on the positive outcome God has promised and repeat it over and over to ourselves until we develop a mental picture of what he wants us to experience. That's precisely the advice God gave Joshua in order to set him on the path to victorious entry into the Promised Land after the Israelites had been trapped in the wilderness for forty years. God described the territory he had promised to the Israelites and told Joshua what their future would be like—he gave Joshua a mental picture of the victories ahead, the lands they would conquer, and the prosperity the Israelites would enjoy. He then called Joshua to constantly think about the promises and laws God gave to Moses at Mount Sinai—which included the promises of prosperity God has just repeated. Joshua was to remind himself over and over about what God had told him so it would remain fresh in his heart and mind.[17]

Just as Joshua was to constantly remind himself of God's promises, so we must keep telling ourselves over and over what God has promised us until we can see it in our mind's eye. For instance, if your marriage is struggling, say to yourself over and over, "I can see my marriage getting better and better until it is everything God wants it to be." If you aren't performing well at your job, repeat to yourself, "I can see myself performing so well that everyone will take notice." If, like me, you're struggling with your weight, recite, as I do every morning, "The spirit of self-control lives with me, enabling me to rule and reign over food." If you've had a serious accident that has left you unable to walk, say to yourself, "I can see myself walking again." Meditate on that. Say it repeatedly until, in your mind's eye, you see yourself walking. No matter what sort of trap you're in, if you do this, God will turn your life around and give you a new direction.

The Bible tells the story of a woman who had a seemingly incurable blood disease (the disease probably involved her monthly cycle, implying it was nearly constant). She'd spent all her money going from one doctor to the next trying to find a cure, but her condition continued to worsen. To compound her distress, in biblical times, if a woman was unclean in this way, her life would be severely restricted. She couldn't get married or, if she was married, enjoy the affection of her spouse: her husband would be forbidden to touch her intimately. She couldn't have children or allow any children she already had to touch her. No one could touch anything she sat on or slept on or wore without becoming ceremonially unclean.[18]

You can imagine the woman's intolerable situation. Not only did she have an incurable disease, but she also would have suffered from a broken heart and wounded spirit because she was condemned to live in virtual isolation. People would avoid her, maybe even shoo her away. Shopkeepers would keep a careful watch over anything she touched, probably wincing if it seemed she might sit down. Her friends, if she had any, would be reluctant to invite her into their homes. They and she would know that such a visit, upon her departure, would set off a flurry of scrubbing, and her chair would have to be hidden away so no one would accidentally sit on it for the remainder of the day. Probably, by this time, the woman had given up on visiting altogether—and her friends had long ago stopped asking.

But worst of all, throughout her day, she would see other women embrace their husbands, other mothers gather their children into their arms. Each time she saw such simple moments of affection, she would have died another death, sinking ever deeper into an abyss of despair. Her life must have been miserable and lonely.

One day she heard that Jesus of Nazareth, the miracle worker, was passing by, and a desperate idea came into her head. She would reach out to Jesus when he passed by, in the hope that he would heal her of her incurable disease. But a huge crowd was following Jesus, making it all but impossible for her to get close to him. Adding to that the fact that she was a woman in a patriarchal society—and a penniless, unclean woman at that—her chances of capturing Jesus' attention must have seemed slim. To make matters worse, he was walking side by side with Jairus, the ruler of the synagogue. Jairus had the authority to order her away before she could even speak to Jesus; what would she do then?

But she didn't give up. She refused to stay in the situation forced on her by circumstance and society. Instead, she acted on faith, deciding in that moment that though she wasn't allowed to touch anyone, she would risk everything to touch Jesus. Perhaps she thought, *If my touch makes people unclean, surely the touch of this holy man will do the opposite!* We don't know if she realized that he was the Messiah, but she seemed to realize that he had the power of God. And in that belief, she focused her attention on his robe. "If only I may touch His garment, I shall be made well,"[19] she said to herself.

On the surface, that would seem like no more than a simple statement; but in the original language, the verse tells us that she *kept on*[20] saying to herself, "If only I may touch His garments, I shall be made well." So we can easily imagine the poor woman's painful progress through the crowd toward Jesus, perhaps on hands and knees, being stepped on and kicked repeatedly. "If only I may touch His garment, I shall be made well. If only I may touch His garment, I shall be made well. If only I may touch His garment, I shall be made well. If only I may touch His garment, I shall be made well."

By using SMART Talk, she was creating a mental image of herself as a cured woman and propelling herself toward that miraculous reality. And the miracle happened! When she reached Jesus and touched his garment, she was instantly cured of her "incurable" disease. She had used her words—her SMART Talk—to free her from her trap and turn her life around. Notice that Jesus even commended her for it: "Be of good cheer, daughter; your faith has made you well."[21] Her mental picture was a form of faith, and God blessed her for it.

One interesting detail from the story confirms the attitude of faith Jesus commended in the woman: the place on the garment for which she reached. Matthew and Luke tell us that she reached for the hem, or "fringe" of his cloak.[22] Why is this significant? Perhaps you've seen pictures of a modern Jewish prayer shawl with long tassels dangling from the corners. Back in the days of Moses, God commanded Jewish men to wear these tassels on the corners of their garments as a reminder of God's covenant with Israel.[23] The tassels were symbols of God's authority and his promise. In Jesus' day, these tassels were sewn onto the hem of a man's outer cloak. Many scholars believe the words *hem* and *fringe* from the story of the sick woman refer to the tassels Jesus wore.[24] If so, the woman was literally reaching for the symbols of God's authority. Her words were not just blind belief or hope but active confirmation of God's promises through the ages. She put her faith in what she knew to be true—that despite all the pain and misery and loneliness of her life, God still loved her and would turn her life around.

AFFIRM YOUR EXPECTATIONS AS IF THEY WERE ALREADY REALIZED

Remember how God speaks. He speaks of nonexistent things as if they already existed;[25] if we're going to imitate God, we must do the same. For example, if we're sick and we believe it is God's will to heal us, based on the promises in his Word,[26] then we need to say to ourselves over and over, "I am healed." If we believe it is God's will to bless us financially, based on the promises in his Word,[27] we need to say, "I have more than I need." If we believe it is God's will for us to lose weight in order to have a healthy body,[28] we need to repeat over and over to ourselves, "I am thin." We are speaking like God by talking about nonexistent things as if they were already real.

I'll share with you a personal story of how this worked in my life—in a way that surprised even me. When my staff and I were planning our church's new building, we flew to Indiana to visit a church built by a construction company we were considering. I don't like flying that much to begin with, but I despise flying on small planes. I want a nice, big, sturdy jumbo jet around me. But the only planes that flew into the airport where we were headed were small propeller planes—puddle jumpers. We flew into a major airport on a jet, but nobody had told me the last hop would be on a small plane; if they had, I wouldn't have gone.

We flew that last leg on a twelve-passenger prop plane. It was so loud inside that we couldn't hear each other talk. We could feel every gust of wind that hit the aircraft. It was forty-five minutes of misery. By the time I got off, I was so sick I couldn't have spent another minute on that plane. My head was spinning, my stomach was in knots, and my loving, caring staff was laughing at me: not one of them had gotten sick.

"We are not going back home on a prop plane," I told them. "I'm going to ask for a different flight that gets us on a big plane."

"Sorry, Frank," one member replied, "but the airline said there are no big planes flying into or out of this airport."

I stared them down. "We are getting a big plane," I repeated. "If you can't believe it with me, then you all just shut up. Don't say a word. I don't want to hear anything negative about it. I will believe God for myself, and you all will just fly on the big plane with me."

They laughed, knowing I was (at least partly) horsing around. But I really did not want to get on another prop plane.

When we returned to the airport from the church, I went to every person behind the counter and asked, "Can you get us on a big plane?"

"I'm sorry, sir, we don't have any big planes that fly in here," was the consistent reply. I'd ask to speak to someone else, and that person would tell me the same thing: big planes did not fly to this airport.

So when the time came for our flight, we climbed aboard another little twelve-passenger puddle jumper like the one we flew in on. We taxied out onto the runway. And sat there. Forty minutes went by, but we didn't take off. Forty minutes turned into an hour and a half. We didn't move. Finally, after two hours, the flight attendant said, "We're sorry, folks, but there's been a problem with this plane, and we can't get it fixed. You'll need to go back into the terminal, and we'll have another plane ready for you soon."

I joked, "See guys? We are getting a big plane! God is going to give us a big plane." My staff laughed at me, insisting, "No, we're not getting a big plane!"

"Yes we are," I said. "I told you, don't say anything negative. We are getting a big plane."

Awhile later, the airline brought out another small plane like the last one. My staff teased me, but I joked back, "Look, this plane isn't going to take off either. We're getting a big plane."

We sat on that plane for about an hour before it started moving down the runway, literally ready to take off. My staff laughed and shouted at me over the noise of the engine, "We told you we weren't getting a bigger plane!"

And then the plane slowed down, turned around, and headed back to the terminal. The pilot apologized, saying another mechanical problem had surfaced and that the airline would make other arrangements for us.

"We're getting a big plane," I told everyone. They laughed, but by now we were all beginning to wonder what was going to happen.

Two hours later, the most marvelous sight I've ever seen came down from the sky—a jumbo jet, arriving to pick us up. We flew out of that airport, the sole eleven passengers on a great big, God-provided plane.

Obviously, the Bible doesn't promise us a jumbo jet whenever we want one. But God does promise to meet our needs, and though I'd been joking (sort of), I think the Lord knew I needed that big plane to calm my fear. And I think he also wanted to give me a story to share with you.

Just as the sick woman did in reaching for Jesus—and even as I did, speaking about the plane—if we are to escape whatever trap we find ourselves in, we must not speak of things as they are but rather as we (and God) intend them to be. If they are SMART words, they call up God's plan and purpose for our lives.

RESPOND TO NEGATIVE TALK
WITH POSITIVE TALK

SMART Talk also involves countering the negative words that so often challenge our pursuit of God's destiny for our lives. Think back once again to how David defeated Goliath. When Saul told David that he couldn't go out and fight the Philistine giant because he was too young and inexperienced to challenge that stronger and more experienced warrior, David countered Saul's negative words with a passionate, positive response: "Your servant has been keeping his father's sheep. When a lion or a bear came and carried off a sheep from the flock, I went after it, struck it and rescued the sheep from its mouth. When it turned on me, I seized it by its hair, struck it and killed it. Your servant has killed both the lion and the bear; this uncircumcised Philistine will be like one of them, because he has defied the armies of the living God. The LORD who delivered me from the paw of the lion and the paw of the bear will deliver me from the hand of this Philistine."[29]

So Saul, impressed by David's courage and positive talk, gave in: "Go, and the LORD be with you!"[30]

Our words must always be positive, because negatives not counteracted with positives remain negative forces that play over and over in our minds and hearts until, eventually, we give in to them. Instead of allowing negative forces to persist, we must respond with positive talk to escape from our trap and turn our lives around.

TAKE CONTROL OF YOUR THOUGHTS

Perhaps the single most important key to effective SMART Talk is taking control of our thoughts. Have you ever noticed that even when you try not to, you tend to say what you've been thinking about? That's because our mouths and our minds are linked, and it explains why it's good advice to think before you speak. I'm sure all of us can recall a time or two when we wish we'd given a little more thought to something before we opened our mouths.

I still cringe inwardly whenever I remember something that happened one Sunday after church, when my wife and I were greeting people in the foyer and a couple we hadn't seen in a while excitedly came over to greet us. Genuinely delighted to see each other again after such a long time, we began to share news, and my wife and I learned that our old friends had recently had a baby and that it was "just the cutest little thing in the world."

At that point—without thinking before speaking—I pointed at the new mother's stomach and enthusiastically exclaimed, "And wow! I see you're about to have another one."

How I wish I could have taken those words back! How I wish I had thought before I spoke. Imagine how embarrassed all of us were when she just looked at me and said, "Oh no. I just haven't lost the extra weight yet from my pregnancy."

That was a bout of foot-in-mouth disease that could have been easily prevented if I had just controlled my thoughts—if I had only thought before speaking.

As the Bible tells us, "Whatever is in your heart determines what you say."[31] So, since there is a mind-mouth connection, we must all take control of our thoughts by "meditating on things true, noble, reputable, authentic, compelling, gracious—the best, not the worst; the beautiful, not the ugly; things to praise, not things to curse."[32] In order to talk SMART, we have to think SMART—which means taking control of what we think by not giving ourselves over to whatever it is that encourages unproductive thoughts.

Talk to Yourself

An effective use of SMART Talk is to talk to ourselves in positive terms. We all have internal dialogue, but too often those conversations with ourselves are negative. We need to talk SMART to ourselves, the way David may have done when he was trapped and discouraged by life—giving himself a pep talk. Perhaps he did this by speaking the end from the beginning, perhaps by muttering over and over to himself until he formed a mental picture of what God wanted for his life, perhaps by affirming what he believed God was going to do as if it were already done, or perhaps by responding to negative thoughts with positive ones. Whatever the form of his internal SMART Talk, it worked. It encouraged him and freed him from his trap of distress. All of us need to talk to ourselves in that way, encouraging ourselves and, as the Bible tells us, "speaking to yourselves in psalms and hymns and spiritual songs, singing and making melody in your heart to the Lord."[33]

The most authoritative voice in our lives is our own voice. We believe it more than we believe any other voice. So we must speak to ourselves, not just saying anything that comes to mind but encouraging ourselves in the Lord. In other words, we must tell ourselves what we know God is saying, not what our wayward thoughts are telling us. We can know the difference by measuring our thoughts against the truth of God's Word. As we've learned, God wants us to imitate him; when we do that, thinking positive thoughts and using SMART Talk in our internal dialogue, wonderful things can happen, as they did when God spoke to himself. When God said to himself, "Let Us make man in Our image, according to Our likeness,"[34] that miracle happened. The genius of his creativity was released, and he created his greatest master-piece—us! Similarly, when we speak to ourselves, we release our creative genius to be and do everything God has created us to be and do. That's when we'll be empowered to escape our trap and turn our lives around.

The WYSIWYG Principle

What is the power behind SMART Talk? Why does it work? Why can God turn our lives around, even when we're trapped, when we use SMART Talk? The answer lies in a principle to which Jesus himself called attention: "Have faith in God. For assuredly, I say to you, whoever says to this mountain, 'Be removed and be cast into the sea,' and does not doubt in his heart, but believes that those things he says will be done, he will have whatever he says. Therefore I say to you, whatever things you ask when you pray, believe that you receive them, and you will have them."[35] Notice that Jesus said we will have whatever we say. I call it the WYSIWYG (wiss´ ē wig) principle—What You *Say* Is What You Get.

In Jesus' response to the disciples' exclamations over the miraculous results (a withered fig tree) that followed one of his commands, he seems to have been answering their unasked question: "How do we get the results you get, Jesus?" His answer: "Have faith in God."

Some Bibles—mine, for instance—have a text note explaining how that answer should be translated from the original language, and here's what it says: "Have the faith of God!"[36] Some people might consider that an impossibility. But it isn't, for two reasons we've already noted: (1) God invites us to imitate him; and (2) God has deposited his ability within us—as the Bible tells us: "By the grace given me I say to every one of you: Do not think of yourself more highly than you ought, but rather think of yourself with sober judgment, in accordance with the measure of faith God has given you."[37]

The specific "measure of faith" God has given us is the ability he has instilled in each of his children. Faith is more than belief; faith is an ability. It is an *empowering* belief. Faith enables us to do things we wouldn't ordinarily be able to do. By faith Abraham was able to father a child when he was nearly a hundred years old. By faith Moses led the Israelites to freedom. By faith David slew Goliath. Faith gives us abilities beyond our natural abilities; it empowers us to do more than we can do naturally. In other words, what that verse is telling us is that without God, you and I are nothing—but that because he has deposited his ability inside each of us, we are something. Since God has put the measure of faith inside each of us, it's possible for us to "have the faith of God."

But how do we release it?

We speak it. Just as God creates through his words, so you and I need to use our words to create what God has destined for us so that he can turn our lives around—even when we're trapped.

SMART Talk Guidelines

I won't lie to you—it can be hard to believe and speak what God says about us and our circumstances. But the WYSIWYG Principle still applies. What we say is what we get, and if we abide by that principle and practice SMART Talk, God will turn our lives around. With that consoling point in mind, let's consider a few rules that we need to keep in mind in order to talk SMART.

DON'T LOSE YOUR BALANCE

The Bible tells us to be well-balanced—temperate and sober of mind.[38] It doesn't teach us that we can just use our words as if they were a sort of magic wand that we can wave to achieve any level of success we desire. You cannot tell yourself over and over that you will be starting pitcher for the Boston Red Sox and expect it to happen if God hasn't given you the talent or skills needed to do so. Your words have to reflect God's purpose for your life. Nor should you expect God to honor talk that is merely selfish or self-glorifying or that violates his Word. Anything we say must be in line with what God promises for our lives. For example, you cannot say that you'll marry someone who is already married and expect God to honor it; it would be outside the boundaries of what his Word promises. We all may want to be billionaires, but just because you say, "I'm going to be a billionaire" and ask God to do it doesn't mean he will make it so.

However, the Bible does say that God promises to meet all our needs according to his riches in glory by Jesus Christ.[39] So if we're struggling financially, we can begin to speak about our financial futures in line with God's Word.

In every need we face, if you and I will accept what God's Word promises us and says about us, and then imitate God's Word in our own thoughts and speech, what he promises for us will come to pass. As Jesus put it, "If you remain in me and my words remain in you, ask whatever you wish, and it will be given you."[40] That's not carte blanche to ask for whatever we want. But it *is* a promise that we may ask for what God wants for us—for he knows what we truly need—and expect God's blessings in return.

How do we discover what God wants for us? As Jesus said, we can remain in him, and his words will remain in us. This happens through prayer and time spent studying God's Word. In fact, one of the best ways to declare the end from the beginning is to find a promise in God's Word and use that scripture as the basis for declaring your future.

Remember the story, from chapter three in this book, of how eagles are trained to hone in on their master's voice? If you want a new direction for your life, tune yourself to hear God's voice through his Word, and soon you'll find yourself speaking God's direction for your life. If you seek God's blessing, align your heart to desire what God desires, and those blessings will come.

FORECAST THE FUTURE

For the WYSIWYG Principle to bring God's turnaround for our lives, we must be more than reporters, just talking about how things are—about how our jobs are in jeopardy, about how our marriages seem beyond repair, about how we're going to die because our doctor tells us we will, about our aches and pains, etc. Sure, it's all right to take our problems to God in prayer. God wants us to do that, and he welcomes it. But after we do that, we must move beyond merely reporting the facts about our situations and begin forecasting the future according to God's plan for our lives.

In Numbers 13 the Bible tells of twelve spies, or members of an advance reconnoitering team. They returned to the Israelite camp after venturing into Canaan to scout out the land prior to the Israelites' entry into the territory God had promised them. In spite of God's promises and the miracles they had seen him do on their behalf, their fear of what they saw in Canaan overpowered their faith, leading them to focus their report on the potential traps— and thereby infecting the hearts of others in the camp with the same misguided fear. The result was a forty-year delay before the Israelites were able to enjoy the realization of God's promise. If those hapless scouts had only had faith and used SMART Talk to forecast success, God would have been able to help them escape from their desert trap and turn their lives around sooner.

TALK TO THE MOUNTAIN

Remember again the words of Jesus in Matthew's gospel, where Jesus gives us the WYSIWYG Principle: "Whoever says to this mountain . . . he will have whatever he says."[41] Notice that Jesus made it clear: if God is going to turn our lives around when we're trapped by mountain-size obstacles, we must not talk *about* our mountain but rather *to* our mountain.

I can think of no better biblical illustration of the WYSIWYG Principle than the story of Babylonian king Nebuchadnezzar and the three captured Hebrew men named Shadrach, Meshach, and Abednego.

King Nebuchadnezzar captured the city of Jerusalem and brought back to Babylon the best and brightest of that city to serve him. Three of the most promising among them—Shadrach, Meshach, and Abednego—were elevated to top positions as administrators in the province of Babylon.[42]

Then one day, emboldened by his ego, Nebuchadnezzar had a golden image ninety feet tall made and set it up in the plain of Dura, where everyone could see and admire it. Nebuchadnezzar clearly commanded that when music was played, all of his subjects were to fall down before it and worship the image. As an encouragement to his subjects to follow his command, Nebuchadnezzar also decreed that those failing to bow down before the statue when they heard the music would be thrown into a fiery furnace and burned alive.

But Shadrach, Meshach, and Abednego obeyed the Word of God[43] rather than the words of Nebuchadnezzar: they refused to bow to the image of gold or worship anyone other than God. When everyone else hit the ground at the sound of the music, the three Hebrew men remained standing. Of course, someone was only too happy to turn them in.

When Nebuchadnezzar learned that someone had dared to defy him, he was enraged. He commanded that the three insubordinate men be brought to him, where he offered to give them one more chance to comply: "Is it true, Shadrach, Meshach and Abednego, that you do not serve my gods or worship the image of gold I have set up? Now when you hear the sound of the horn, flute, zither, lyre, harp, pipes and all kinds of music, if you are ready to fall down and worship the image I made, very good. But if you do not worship it, you will be thrown immediately into a blazing furnace. Then what god will be able to rescue you from my hand?"[44]

Faced with a trap that seemed inescapable, Shadrach, Meshach, and Abednego began to tap into the power of SMART Talk. Instead of giving up or using their mouths to spout DUMB Talk, throwing verbal rocks back at their accusers, they spoke directly to their mountain-size problem, holding on to their faith in God to deliver them from their trap and turn their lives around.

Shadrach, Meshach, and Abednego answered the king: "O Nebuchadnezzar, we have no need to answer you in this matter. If that is the case, our God whom we serve is able to deliver us from the burning fiery furnace, and He will deliver us from your hand, O king. But if not, let it be known to you, O king, that we do not serve your gods, nor will we worship the gold image which you have set up."[45]

BE GOVERNED BY CONFIDENCE, NOT COMPROMISE

The three Jews were governed by confidence, not compromise. They didn't say to themselves, "Okay, let's just bow down and save our hides. After all, God knows our hearts; he knows that we don't really worship this image. He knows we love him. And surely God doesn't want us to die in a fiery furnace. So, just this once, we can compromise."

Compromise doesn't work, though. Compromise kills confidence. We must talk confidently to our problem, and to do so, we must avoid compromise. Remember what the three trapped Jews said to Nebuchadnezzar: "Our God whom we serve is able to deliver us from the burning fiery furnace, and He will deliver us from your hand."[46] They looked at their problem and said, in essence, "We have a God who makes that ninety-foot-high statue look puny.

We have a God who by his Word brought the universe into existence, brought order to the earth, hung the stars in the sky, put the planets in their orbits, and created the sun and the moon. We have a God who commanded the sea to stop at the shoreline and whose mere words open the eyes of the blind, unstop deaf ears, and strengthen crippled legs."

Yet then they continued with, "But if not, let it be known to you, O king, that we do not serve your gods, nor will we worship the gold image which you have set up."[47]

Nebuchadnezzar threw them into the blazing furnace.

Shadrach, Meshach, and Abednego had done their part by speaking to their mountain; it was then up to God to turn their lives around by rescuing them from the fiery trap they were in. And he did. As soon as the three men were thrown into the furnace, Nebuchadnezzar was shocked by what he saw. "King Nebuchadnezzar was astonished; and he rose in haste and spoke, saying to his counselors, 'Did we not cast three men bound into the midst of the fire?' They answered and said to the king, 'True, O king.' 'Look!' he answered, 'I see four men loose, walking in the midst of the fire; and they are not hurt, and the form of the fourth is like the Son of God.' "[48]

You see, when you talk about your God to your problem, God shows up in the middle of your trap and turns your life around! Our words allow God to act on our behalf. Notice that Shadrach, Meshach, and Abednego got exactly what they said. They said, "If you throw us in, our God will be able to save us from the fiery furnace." And that's exactly what happened!

If we do as Shadrach, Meshach, and Abednego did and practice tongue control, allow ourselves to be governed by confidence rather than by compromise, and speak directly to our problem about our God—in other words, if we talk SMART—then God can deliver us from whatever trap we may be in and turn our lives around.

8

HOLDING FAST AS YOU
WEATHER LIFE'S STORMS

Have you ever been caught in a sudden storm? It's a beautiful day, the sun is shining, and it feels like nothing could possibly go wrong on this day. Sure, there's a cloud over there on the horizon, but it's no big deal—and then *BOOM!* Thunder crashes, lightning seems to crack open the sky, and rain pours down. The winds are blowing, the sunshine is gone, and you're out there, exposed, with nowhere to hide from nature's wrath. You wonder, *What happened? Where did this storm come from? How did I get caught in this? What am I going to do?*

I know of a young woman who loves to run. A few years ago she was living in Memphis, Tennessee, and went for a run on a beautiful summer morning. Now when she runs, she runs a long way—she was a cross-country track star in high school and college. To her, running several miles is like a stroll around the block. She thinks nothing of it—so little, in fact, that she often pays little attention to where she happens to be when she's running. So on this particular morning, she had been running for a while and, without thinking about it, had entered a neighborhood where she knew no one. Suddenly the wind began to blow harder and harder, turning into a raging windstorm—the kind meteorologists refer to as a *derecho* because it involves straight-line winds rather than the more familiar circular winds of a tornado. It turned out to be one of the worst windstorms to hit Memphis in a hundred years, with gusts of over a hundred miles an hour—"Hurricane Elvis," the locals later dubbed it. The storm uprooted trees and street signs, tore the roofs off buildings, knocked down power lines, and did millions of dollars of damage throughout the city, even killing two people[1]—and this young woman was out in the middle of it.

She's a petite woman; to the wind she might as well have been a piece of paper. When she realized her danger, she began banging on doors, looking for shelter. But whether because she was a stranger or because people were still in bed or had retreated to safe areas of their homes to ride out the storm, none of the residents came to their doors. In desperation she grabbed the nearest tree and pressed herself against it, praying for rescue. The woman was terrified that she might be struck by debris or swept away herself by the raging storm. Just as the wind was reaching its peak, a woman saw her through a window and came out to help her inside to safety.

Storms Will Come

Life can be like that. Just like that young woman, we're running along as we always do, thinking everything is fine, and *WHAM!*— we're caught in a storm. Maybe you lose your job, or the debt you've been ignoring suddenly becomes too large to handle. Maybe your spouse walks in with divorce papers, your kid winds up in trouble, or you learn you have cancer. Whatever the cause of your storm, your life is in turmoil, and you're in danger. The winds rage around you, you don't know where to turn, and you're terrified that no one will rescue you. I've felt that way. I began this book by describing to you just such a storm in my life as I struggled to deal with the financial pressures in my ministry and my business—a storm that raged for fourteen months.

Storms come in many varieties, and no one is exempt from them—not the great or the small, not the rich or the poor, not the educated or the uneducated—not even the believer or the nonbeliever. Just as meteorologists classify storms (hurricanes, tornados, derechos, and so on), so we can classify life storms into five types: satanic storms, sudden storms, self-made storms, storms by association, and sovereign storms.

1. SATANIC STORMS

Satanic storms happen because we have an enemy named Satan who loves to intrude into our lives, as the Bible admonishes us: "Be self-controlled and alert. Your enemy the devil prowls around like a roaring lion looking for someone to devour."[2] A satanic storm is what we usually think of as a tragedy—the death of a child, a terminal illness that arises despite our efforts at healthy living, or a tragedy resulting from a deliberate act of malice, such as crime or sin inflicted on us. The individuals affected by the terrorist attacks on September 11, 2001, were clearly assaulted by a satanic storm. These are the storms that may cause us to doubt God or question his authority and his love, or to turn away from the wisdom of his Word. When storms like these happen, watch out! In that moment, it's important to look to God more than ever, because your enemy is trying to make you look away.

2. SUDDEN STORMS

Sudden storms occur because we live in a fallen world where the effects of sin cause storms to erupt without apparent cause or reason. These storms come without warning, striking us from out of the blue.

- Your boss calls you into her office and says the company is closing your department and laying you off.
- Your carefully planned investments go south because of a stock-market crash.
- Despite all your healthy habits, a routine physical reveals a lump in your breast.

Whatever the cause or their nature, sudden storms catch us off guard and unprepared and throw us into turmoil.

3. SELF-MADE STORMS

Self-made storms happen because of our own poor decisions. They can result from immoral choices and sin, such as the one-night stand that destroys a marriage. But they can also come from choices we make out of foolishness or ignorance—signing a contract without reading it carefully or going into credit-card debt because we overspent. Whatever the specific nature of the storm, we've caused it through our own actions or inactions. These are the storms that can trigger feelings of guilt or shame.

4. STORMS BY ASSOCIATION

Storms by association strike not because of bad decisions we've made, but because of bad decisions by others whose lives are intertwined with ours:

- Your boss engages in financial improprieties, bankrupting the company, and now you're out of a job.

- Your business partner embezzled money and lied to the IRS, so suddenly your reputation and livelihood are on the line.
- Your husband cheated on you, so your marriage is in turmoil.
- Your kid gets in a car with some friends who'd been drinking, and you get a call from the police or the hospital.

You've done nothing to cause these storms—you may even have done everything right—but someone else's choice has turned your world upside down.

5. SOVEREIGN STORMS

Sovereign storms are markedly different. God himself brings these storms into our lives, not to hurt us, but to make us think, test us, and ultimately help us. Sovereign storms may revolve around an opportunity to choose right from wrong: we can compromise, take the easy way, and get something we desire; or we can do the right thing, knowing that it's going to take us longer to achieve our desired result. Often these are storms we encounter when stubbornness and pride are preventing us from submitting to God's will for our lives. Jonah is a perfect example of this.[3] He disobeyed God's instructions to go and preach to the Ninevites and, instead, set sail for Tarshish, a city far from Nineveh in the opposite direction.

Remember Your Ally

Sometimes a storm may seem to have several causes. But the most important thing to know about a storm isn't its cause; far more important is knowing how to thrive in the midst of life's storms and overcome them. The way to do that is by forming an alliance with God, who can turn our lives around in spite of any storm we might encounter.

That's exactly what the apostle Paul did when his ship was caught in a terrible storm as he was sailing to Rome to be tried before Caesar. Paul knew something we all need to know about overcoming life's storms: God is an ally we can't do without. Paul knew, as did the psalmist, that "My help comes from the LORD."[4] Paul knew that no matter how bad things look, no matter where the storm we find ourselves in came from or what its cause, God is our ally and the source of our help. As Paul himself wrote, "If God is for us, who can be against us?"[5]

Commenting on that verse, Max Lucado once wrote:

> God is for you. Not "may be," not "has been," not "was," not "would be," but "God is!" He is for you. Today. At this hour. At this minute. As you read this sentence. No need to wait in line or come back tomorrow. He is with you. He could not be closer than he is at this second. His loyalty won't increase if you are better nor lessen if you are worse. He is for you.
>
> God is *for* you. Turn to the sidelines; that's God cheering your run. Look past the finish line; that's God applauding your steps. Listen for him in the bleachers, shouting your name. Too tired to continue? He'll carry you. Too discouraged to fight? He's picking you up. God is *for* you.
>
> God is for *you*. Had he a calendar, your birthday would be circled. If he drove a car, your name would be on his bumper. If there's a tree in heaven, he's carved your name in the bark. We know he has a tattoo, and we know what it says: 'I have written your name on my hand,' he declares (Isa. 49:16).[6]

Since God is for us, it's God with whom we should ally ourselves in the midst of life's storms. When we do that, God can turn our lives around and give us a new direction.

Unfortunately, though, when we make an alliance with God in the midst of a storm and things don't change quickly in our favor, we're sometimes tempted to break the alliance and do things our own way. We feel that we've given God a chance, and he hasn't come through for us.

I'll share an example from my own life when I forgot who my ally was and needed a reminder. In chapter six I told you about my experience working four jobs to support my family during my early days as an assistant pastor. That was a miserable time for me—a storm whose cause I could only place at the feet of God. I remember I was in my home office—not a fancy office, just a corner in an unfinished basement where I had set up a desk and a chair—and I was writing out checks to pay our bills. This always made me miserable because there was never enough money to pay them all. Even though I was working as much as I could and planning as carefully as I could, I always ended up in a bind. I remember saying, "God, it isn't supposed to be like this. I left a well-paying career as a CPA for you. My wife left a well-paying job as a day-care teacher so we could move here. We left a brand-new home that was being built for us to go into ministry and serve you. You say in your Word that 'Everyone who has left houses or brothers or sisters or father or mother or children or fields for my sake will receive a hundred times as much and will inherit eternal life.'[7] But here I am, serving you, having to work four jobs, and I don't have enough money to pay my bills. Sometimes I don't even have enough money to buy diapers and formula for my new baby or food to put on the table."

I remember what an awful feeling that was, like God had abandoned me in that storm. And then I felt God telling me to get up from my desk. He told me to turn around and look around that basement. In another corner was a brand-new television. And I sensed God asking me, *Where did you get that television?*

"It was a gift," I said.

Then I felt God leading me to open the door into the part of our basement that was our garage. I looked at the used car parked there. *And that?* God asked.

"It was a gift," I answered.

The Lord led me upstairs, into the living room, where I could see our furniture—all new. *And these, Frank?*

"Those were gifts, Lord."

We went on through every room in the house. Our bedroom, my son's room with his new baby furniture, the kitchen with the microwave, the stove, the refrigerator—all gifts from friends and family. We had not needed to pay for a single one.

Soon I was opening drawers and cabinets, looking at plates, coffee cups, knives, forks—it seemed that everything we owned had been given to us. Before long I was holding up spoons and saying, "Thank you for this spoon, Lord!" I went from counting my miseries, which were few, to counting my blessings, which were many. All along, in the middle of that storm of financial struggle, God had been my ally. I just needed to be reminded.

Stick with Your Ally

Let's put ourselves in the apostle Paul's shoes. As we come to Acts 27 in the Bible, we read about Paul's boarding a ship on what he believed would be an important mission. God had said that Paul would preach the message of Christ before kings,[8] and Paul was about to embark on a voyage to Rome. Although he was a prisoner being sent to plead his case before Caesar, the most powerful world leader of the time, Paul was prepared to seize the great opportunity it provided to share the good news of faith in Jesus. Perhaps Paul understood the significance of this mission: Caesar came to Christ, it seems logical that it would be just a matter of time before Christianity would spread throughout the Roman Empire and countless people's lives would be changed.

You'd think that when someone was obeying God and following his plan, God would at least make sure things went smoothly. We all know, though, that things don't always turn out the way we plan or anticipate. We can count on meeting with bumps, twists, and turns in the road, as well as unexpected developments.

Right from the start, Paul's voyage never went smoothly. It was late in the sailing season, and the winds were against the ship, which slowed it down. They had to skirt the southern coast of Crete rather than head straight for Rome. The delay caused them to lose much time, and when they reached the port of Fair Havens, only halfway along the coast of the island, they were past the season for safe travel by sea. Although Paul warned the men that disaster would surely overtake them should they continue their journey, endangering ship, cargo, and their own lives, no one listened to him. "Since the harbor was unsuitable to winter in, the majority decided that we should sail on, hoping to reach Phoenix and winter there. . . . When a gentle south wind began to blow, they thought they had obtained what they wanted; so they weighed anchor and sailed along the shore of Crete."[9]

The gentle south wind, however, soon turned into something else. Before long a wind of hurricane force, called a northeaster—the kind of winter storm all sailors fear and few survive—caught the ship and drove it violently along. Wind and waves battered the ship. Doing everything they could to survive, the sailors passed ropes under the craft to keep it from breaking apart. They tossed the ship's cargo into the sea to lighten the load, and the next day they even tossed overboard the ship's tackle (planks, spars, and maybe even the yardarm with the mainsail attached) to keep from being dragged to the bottom of the sea. Acts 20:20 records the depths of the sailors' despair: "When neither sun nor stars appeared for many days and the storm continued raging, we finally gave up all hope of being saved."

Intense, long-lasting storms can shake us and cause us to lose hope, but only if we let our fear draw our focus away from our ally, God. We can imagine the kind of panic that must have beset those sailors, and we can imagine the kind of struggle going on in the mind and heart of Paul. I'm sure he was plagued by the same kind of questions that assail all of us during life's storms, making us doubt the value of serving God or doing things his way if our present suffering is an example of what we can expect to get in return.

How often do we forget what God has done for us during earlier storms? We go through one storm, and God rescues us, but when we hit the next storm, we don't have faith that he can or will do it again. We start frantically looking for some other solution, forgetting the ally who has helped us before. We abandon that alliance for something immediate, foolishly choosing that which appears strong, yet isn't, over the God who is always strong, no matter how things seem.

When the winds and waves of life's storms assail us; when we're frightened, exhausted, and overwhelmed; when all hope seems gone, it's human nature to forget everything but the storm and the danger. So how can we remember and stick with our ally, even amid life's most terrible storms? Here are four keys to help us cling to our best ally, God.

KEY 1: HOLD FAST TO GOD'S WORD

When the storm hit, Paul remembered that God is our source of help in the midst of every storm. He made use of the first important key to keeping an alliance with God—he held fast to God's word to him. God's words of encouragement helped Paul to believe, when circumstances looked grim, that he and his shipmates would be saved. "Last night an angel of the God whose I am and whom I serve stood beside me and said, 'Do not be afraid, Paul. You must stand trial before Caesar; and God has graciously given you the lives of all who sail with you.' So keep up your courage, men, for I have faith in God that it will happen just as he told me."[10]

God's Word is a lifeline to which we must cling whatever the tempest around us. No matter what conditions are like in the midst of the storm, we can boldly say with Paul, "I have faith in God that it will happen just as he told me."

On our honeymoon, my wife and I found a place nearby where we could rent horses to ride on the beach. We eagerly anticipated what we'd seen of such things on television: romantic shots of a couple riding through the surf with loose-fitting clothing blowing in the wind, their hair bouncing in slow motion and reflecting the tropical sun. We decided we would spend our day on a romantic ride, just the two of us.

The first thing we learned when we arrived at the stable was that everyone goes out in groups. We would have no romantic time alone. So that put a damper on our plans right from the start. But we decided to stick with it, because riding horses is supposed to be fun. Maybe we couldn't be romantic, but we could have a good time.

The guides brought out our horses—mine was named Dino— and led us down the trail to the beach. This trail was winding and narrow, with brush on either side that rose about eight feet high, so the horses moved at a slow walk. I was third in line, and the trail was long. Pretty soon I was starting to feel sore from bumping along in the saddle. Holding on to hope, I thought: *Well, this isn't much fun, but when we get to the beach, it'll be better.*

What they didn't tell me was that Dino was used to being first in the line. I had no clue, and on the trail, there was nothing he could do about it. But when we got to the clearing at the beach, Dino took off racing like you wouldn't believe. It felt to me like he was going a hundred miles an hour. I had no idea how to control this creature. I started yanking on the reins shouting, "Whoa, Dino! Slow down,

Dino! Whoa! Whoa!" pulling back with all my weight, but this horse was not slowing down. I was bouncing around all over his back, the guide was racing after us, and to keep from falling off, I had to hook my arms around the horse's neck. In that moment, all I could do was hold on for dear life and trust the guide to come rescue me.

That's pretty much what Paul did. He kept his faith in the midst of the storm and retained his alliance with God by holding fast to God's word. Just like Paul, we can hold fast to God's Word and have faith that he will come to our rescue. He will be true to his Word and help us through the storm or out of the storm—whichever he chooses. If you're in a financial storm and you've been praying repeatedly for God's blessings, hold on to God's promise, spoken through Paul: "My God shall supply all your need according to His riches in glory by Christ Jesus."[11] If you're in a marital storm, hold on to God's Word, where he says: "What God has joined together, let man not separate."[12] If you're in a physical storm and you've been praying for God to heal your illness, hold on to God's Word that says: "By his wounds you have been healed."[13]

Holding fast to God's word of promise turned Paul's fear into faith. But it didn't stop the storm. Finally, around midnight on the fourteenth night of their wild struggle to survive, the exhausted but seasoned sailors sensed they were approaching land—though they could see nothing through the darkness and the water. When their instruments proved their instincts correct, they began to fear that the wind and waves would drive them to their death, dashing them upon the rocks along the coast, so they dropped four anchors and prayed for daylight.

I love that Paul's second declaration of faith in God's promise to save them, "Not one of you will lose a single hair from his head,"[14] comes on the heels of Paul's telling the men on the ship to eat some food, because the food we need when we're caught in a storm is the

Word of God. Holding fast to God's Word provides the anchor that keeps us safe in the midst of even the most powerful storm.

The eyewitness account continues: "When daylight came, they did not recognize the land, but they saw a bay with a sandy beach, where they decided to run the ship aground if they could. Cutting loose the anchors, they left them in the sea and at the same time untied the ropes that held the rudders. Then they hoisted the fore-sail to the wind and made for the beach. But the ship struck a sand-bar and ran aground. The bow stuck fast and would not move, and the stern was broken to pieces by the pounding of the surf."[15] The ship snapped in half, making it look as if Paul and everyone else on board might die. Yet Paul still held fast to God's word—the double promise that he would preach the gospel before Caesar and that neither Paul nor any of the men aboard would lose their lives. Faith in those promises empowered the apostle to hang on and fight instead of abandoning hope.

As the ship broke apart, those who could swim swam hard for the shore, while those who could not swim grabbed onto planks or pieces of the ship and floated safely to shore. Undoubtedly encouraged by Paul's assurances from God and the food they'd eaten at his insistence, the men either swam or held on—none gave up. You see, that's the power of the Word of God in the midst of life's storms: it gives us staying power. It prevents us from quitting on God and giving up on his promises. It empowers us to swim and to hold on, even when all hell is breaking loose around us, no matter what kind of storms beset us—actual storms like the one Paul and the crew faced, or figurative storms: marital, financial, physical, emotional, or spiritual. When the storms of life strike, sometimes holding on is all we can do. As Paul discovered, though, after we've done everything we know to do, we can count on the help that comes from holding fast to the Word of God. I love the way the old hymn puts that truth:

Standing, standing,
Standing on the promises of God my Savior;
tanding, standing,
I'm standing on the promises of God.

Standing on the promises that cannot fail,
When the howling storms of doubt and fear assail,
By the living word of God I shall prevail,
Standing on the promises of God.

Paul stood on God's promise to him. He held fast to God's word, kept his faith in God, and didn't break his alliance with his only true source of help. Hanging on to the word of God and the floating boards from the ship that had snapped in half, Paul and everyone else who had been on the ship made it safely to land.

KEY 2: SHAKE OFF YOUR PROBLEM

Although Paul and his men were no longer at the mercy of the turbulent sea, Paul's storm hadn't yet ended. When Paul and his crew reached land, they were met by islanders who greeted them warmly. They built a fire to warm the shipwrecked men because, although they were on land, the storm still raged: it was rainy and cold. To help out, Paul gathered a pile of brushwood for the fire. Perhaps he was finally starting to relax, perhaps thinking, *We're on shore! We're finally safe, and we're going to have a nice, warm fire. Thank God! It's over.*

But as Paul was placing the branches on the fire, a viper—a venomous snake—sank its fangs into Paul's hand, injecting its poisonous venom, and even fastening itself firmly to his hand![16]

The snakebite didn't even seem to faze Paul. He just shook off the snake into the fire. Paul knew the second key: we must shake off our problems.

Obviously Paul had learned to trust God's word in any storm. But it's easy to understand the reaction of the people of Malta when they saw Paul struck by the snake: "When the islanders saw the snake hanging from his hand, they said to each other, 'This man must be a murderer; for though he escaped from the sea, Justice has not allowed him to live.' "[17] They were judging Paul in much the same way many of us sometimes presume to stand in judgment of others who are suffering, believing they're being divinely punished for something they've done.

But before we dare to judge others, we must bear in mind that suffering is not always punishment for sin. The causes of Paul's suffering—the storm and the snakebite—weren't the results of something he'd done wrong, but rather of something he was doing right. Paul was following God's plan that he should preach before Caesar and influence a nation, and the devil didn't like it.

We're all guilty of doing wrong things, of course; but sometimes we find ourselves in a storm not because we've done something wrong, but because we're doing something right. We understand that doing wrong should have consequences, but sometimes we're surprised to discover that doing right has consequences too—at times, consequences we don't like.

Sometimes we can see those consequences coming: for example, if your boss asks you to falsify a report to please the company executives, you know that refusing will damage your relationship with him. Hopefully, you'd choose to stand up for what's right anyway and be prepared for the fallout. But sometimes, as with Paul, the trouble doesn't seem connected. You loan money to help a friend out with his rent, and the next day your car breaks down, and you could really use that money for the expensive repair. You join a food drive to supply meals to the elderly, and while you're making your rounds, you get a nail in your tire. These are the moments that make you want to scream, "Life's just not fair!" They can make you believe the old lie "No good deed goes unpunished."

It's times like these when we need to be especially careful not to turn away from God.

Remember that day in my basement, when the viper of my bills jumped up and bit me? I allowed myself to become focused on the negative—to protest, "It's not fair!" But as God reminded me that day, we can't allow ourselves to be distracted by negative events. We must shake them off. If we do, God will turn our lives around.

Things certainly seemed to be going from bad to worse for Paul, as they often do during life's storms. Remember, however, that although things often do get worse before they get better, they *will* get better if we hold fast to the Word of God.

So what about Paul and his viper? Did Paul cry out, "Lord, this just is not fair! How could this happen to me? I just got everybody off the boat, I'm helping pick up some firewood, and this snake bites me! How could you let that happen? Now I'm going to die!" Nope. Paul didn't say anything at all. Acts tells us: "Paul shook the snake off into the fire and suffered no ill effects."[18] He shook it off! Paul knew his God was more powerful than any snake, whether the devil sent it or not. He didn't even blink—he just shook it into the fire and went on doing what God wanted him to do. We, too, must learn to shake things off, because it's crucial to overcoming life's storms.

I'm a baseball coach, and I often have to deal with kids who get hit by pitches. Naturally, I make certain they're physically okay; but once I'm assured of that, I also encourage them to shake off the experience and get back in the game. That's important, because if they don't—if they sit there and think about the pain—they'll become afraid of the ball, and it will affect their ability to play.

As I write this, my son is nine years old. He is a sports phenomenon—and I'm not just bragging because I'm his dad. He's been switch-hitting since he was five. He can hit the ball from both sides of the plate, and he's incredible.

Last year, he faced live pitching for the first time. He was at bat, and he took one in the ribs from a kid who threw pretty hard. My son cried, but he tried to shake it off. He ran to first base and seemed okay. He even batted again and got a hit. So I thought, *Okay, he's past it.*

But the pain stayed with him. The next day, his ribs hurt. The next week, his ribs still hurt. The week after that, his ribs hadn't stopped hurting. I began to worry that he had an injury, but we couldn't find anything wrong. His ribs hurt for almost a month. The pain finally did go away, but not his memory of it. He couldn't shake it off, and at this point in time, he doesn't want to play baseball again.

When we can't shake things off, it can paralyze us or make us give up. But there are things we can do to imitate Paul and give ourselves the ability to shake off the vipers in our lives:

Stop telling everybody your problems.

It's okay, even good, to share what's going on with caring friends, but we don't need to moan to everybody who will listen. There's a time for us to talk, and there's a time for us to listen. When you're sick and you go to the doctor, naturally, you start out by telling the doctor what's wrong. But when you're done, you don't start retelling the problem. You listen to his or her advice so you can get better. And you don't leave the doctor's office and start telling the receptionist what's wrong. You don't tell the parking-garage attendant what's wrong. You don't tell the mail carrier what's wrong. You listen to the doctor's advice, and you follow it. So by all means, share your problems with God. But then stop talking and listen for his reply.

Start talking about what's right.

Join my "basement blessings" routine. The ancient Jews used to say little prayers blessing God for everything—they blessed God when they got dressed, they blessed God when they ate, they blessed God when they worked. As a result, they spent each day reminding themselves of what was good in their lives, and from whom it all came.[19] When you're in the midst of a storm, try focusing on the good God has done for you in the past and is doing for you right now.

Stop hitting rewind.

The worst mistake we make when dealing with a painful event is to keep reliving it. You may be old enough to remember the old introduction to *ABC's Wide World of Sports*. As a montage of sports footage appeared on the screen, narrator Jim McKay extolled the wonders of sports, always repeating the phrase, "The thrill of victory . . . and the agony of defeat." The image that appeared for "the agony of defeat" was a ski jumper falling at the last second of the jump and tumbling off the ski ramp, bouncing against the structure as his limbs flailed and his skis snapped. It always looked incredibly painful, and every time I saw it, I winced. The incident happened in 1970, but years later I and television audiences everywhere still cringed as if it were happening right then.

We do the same thing in life, replaying old hurts over and over and over again in our minds. *Why did she do that to me? Why did that have to happen? If only I hadn't lost that job! If only I hadn't made that mistake!* Those "why dids" and "if onlys" keep us from shaking things off. We have to choose to hit Stop on our mental video player, rip out the tape of our pain, and throw it away.

Purposefully think about other things.

The best way to end that constant playback is to choose to put other images and ideas in our minds—and not just any old thing. The Scriptures tells us: "You'll do best by filling your minds and meditating on things true, noble, reputable, authentic, compelling, gracious—the best, not the worst; the beautiful, not the ugly; things to praise, not things to curse."[20] We can control what we think about.

We can try to focus on good things in our lives or events that brought us joy; in so doing, we change the channel in our minds.

Choose what you let in your gates.

Like ancient watchmen guarding the city gates so no enemy could enter, we need to guard our personal "gates"—our eyes and ears—to make certain that what enters our minds through them is beneficial to us. If we're struggling through a divorce, then we probably shouldn't be watching movies about marriages that break up. We don't need something that's going to trigger our Rewind button. Instead, we should seek out ideas and images that help us think in a different way, that guide us toward real solutions. "If anything is excellent or praiseworthy—think about such things."[21]

Don't do things that reinflict the pain.

Just as we should stop hitting Rewind, letting into our minds images and ideas that trigger our pain, we should also stop repeating harmful actions. Do you remember the joke about the guy who goes to the doctor, jabs his finger in his stomach and says, "Doc, it hurts when I do this"? The doctor replies, "Then don't do that." That's good advice when trying to shake off the vipers of pain in our lives—stop jabbing yourself where it hurts!

Make a decision.

That's it. Just make a decision. When we go through life's storms, we should come to the place where we say, "You know what? I'm not going to let this ruin my life. I'm not going to give it undue time or attention." And then we begin to do things we enjoy, things that bring us blessings from God. We get back to work. We get back to our hobbies. We get involved with a group at our church or join a community activity. We spend time helping others. We deliberately put our minds and our energies into other things. We get up, shake it off, and get back to living out our purpose for God—we accept the direction he has for us, and we move on.

Just as Paul did when the viper struck him, when a storm strikes us and things seem to be going from bad to worse, we must rise up and shake it off.

- We can't allow storms to stop us. Shake them off!
- We can't let storms disturb our sleep. Shake them off!
- We can't permit storms to destroy our marriages and break up our families. Shake them off!
- We can't allow storms to prevent us from pursuing our divine destinies. Shake them off!

The good news is that we can all shake things off when we hold fast to God's Word.

KEY 3: RECOGNIZE THAT GOD TURNS DELAYS INTO DIVINE APPOINTMENTS

When Paul was bitten by the snake, the islanders thought, *Aha! This bad man is now going to die.* The people expected him to swell up or suddenly fall dead, but after waiting a long time and seeing nothing unusual happen to him, they changed their minds and decided he must be a god.[22] They were obviously impressed and amazed by Paul's godlike ability to shake off disaster.

Even though Paul had survived a storm and a snakebite, he still may have been discouraged by the serious delay in his carrying out God's mission for him—to reach Rome and preach to Caesar. But shaking things off, he held fast to God's word and kept in mind that God turns delays into divine appointments. This is the third key.

While I was an assistant pastor, I began to feel strongly that I needed to preach more—not necessarily in the church I was serving, because I always understood that preaching is the senior pastor's job. However, I had a burden and a desire to preach. I started praying, asking God for that opportunity. But the opportunities weren't forthcoming. I felt like I was in a holding pattern, and I began to think, *Maybe I should ask the pastor if I could go to different churches and preach once a month.* But something inside made me hesitate and stay put.

Three months later, I became the senior pastor of the church. If I had jumped the gun, I might have missed God's divine appointment for me.

Think about that idea of divine appointments as we consider what happened next for Paul. A nearby estate belonged to Publius, the chief official of the island. He welcomed Paul and his traveling companions to his home and entertained them hospitably for three days. Publius's father was sick in bed with a fever and dysentery—a potentially deadly combination. Paul went to see him and prayed for him, and the man was healed. When word of this spread, other sick people came to Paul and were also healed.[23]

So there was Paul, who probably had thought he would already be in Rome preaching to Caesar but instead found himself delayed by a hurricane, a shipwreck, and a snakebite. He could have interpreted the delay as a denial from God. He might have looked at these twists in the road as the end of the road. He could have said to himself, *Well, when it rains, it pours.* Instead, he chose to believe that when it pours, God reigns! Paul held fast to his alliance with God, knowing that God can turn delays into divine appointments. He knew that God uses delays to build us, even if they seem bound to break us; and that God uses delays to make us better, even if they were sent by the enemy to make us bitter. Paul chose to hold on to his alliance with God, knowing that God was turning these delays into divine appointments. God had used the unexpected delay to bring revival to the island of Malta!

Like Paul, we must avoid seeing our storms as setbacks and start seeing them as setups for a comeback. Robert Schuller wrote:

There was a young man who died in his early thirties after a brief public career had brought him fame in his time and territory. The tragic element of his life story is that after stunning success, he was falsely accused of a crime that resulted in his imprisonment, trial, and execution. The death penalty was carried out. The end of his life was utter disgrace, humiliation, and shame. I weep as I think of the whole sad, sordid spectacle of that social injustice, except that his name was eventually vindicated. He came back, and his comeback was stunning and spectacular. His honor was restored and elevated. His name today is the most respected and renowned name in the Christian world. Today we even count the years by him, the time before his death and the time after his death. He is the King of Comebacks. His name is Jesus, and he is committed to your comeback![24]

A pastor friend of mine founded a church several years ago with three other people. After about three years of constant work, the church had only about fifty attendees. My friend was discouraged because he'd anticipated that the church would grow more in that amount of time. He still had to work a full-time job in addition to his ministry because the church was too small to afford a full-time salary.

During this time of discouragement, he was offered the opportunity to pastor another church. It wasn't a large church by any means, but it was able to pay him a full-time salary. He visited the church, preached, and thought he had been well received. He felt certain he had the job. But the congregation voted to look for someone else. The door closed completely. Though he'd been fervently praying for such an opportunity, it seemed God hadn't answered.

But my friend decided to pray about the situation again and listen to what God said to his heart. When he did, he came to the conclusion that having that door close was a good thing. He loved the church he had started, and though it was small and couldn't pay him, in his heart he knew it was the place God had for him. He decided to embrace God's delay and see what the Lord had to offer.

Not long after this, God sent some new members to the church who quickly showed themselves to be natural leaders. My friend had borne the leadership responsibility alone until then, as he had no one who was truly able to assist him. These new leaders stepped up as assistant pastors, and the church began to grow. Within a few months the church was large enough to offer my friend a full-time salary; he could quit his other job and devote his time to the ministry he loved. Along with this change, the church began to attract interest from people throughout the community, including some local businessmen and a professional athlete. As a result of their generosity, donations soared, allowing my friend to add much-needed staff and expand the church's ministry even more.

Within six months, my friend went from disappointment to amazement, all because he was willing to accept a divine delay and allow God to turn a temporary setback into an incredible comeback.

I don't know what kind of storm or setback has hit or will hit your life, but I do know that if you'll stick with God, if you'll keep your alliance with him, he'll turn that setback into a setup for a comeback. He'll turn that delay into a divine appointment.

KEY 4: REALIZE THAT GOD'S FAVOR NEVER FAILS

The mother of a friend of mine was flying to Connecticut to visit him. She's an elderly woman, and she didn't know where her seat was on the plane. She wanted an aisle seat because she had an overactive bladder and frequently needed to use the restroom but didn't want to disturb other passengers. She explained her situation to the airline gate attendant and asked if they could move her to an aisle seat. The attendant promised that they would try to make arrangements for her if she would wait while the plane boarded.

So my friend's mother sat patiently while the other passengers got on the plane. After a while, she became concerned: no one had come back to speak to her, and it looked as if almost all the passengers had boarded. So she asked the attendant again, "Did you forget about me? Can you make sure I get an aisle seat?" The attendant politely reassured her, "Ma'am, don't worry, we're still checking people in, and if we have an aisle seat open, we'll change your seat."

The woman sat down again and waited. Finally they motioned for her to come on the plane. But when she got on, she discovered she still didn't have an aisle seat. Disappointed, she took her seat in coach while other passengers stowed their luggage. After everyone was seated, the flight attendant approached the woman and said, "Ma'am, can you come with me?"

The woman worried that she was in trouble for pestering them about the aisle seat. "Did I do anything wrong?" she asked fearfully.

"No ma'am!" the stewardess laughed. "It's just that the only aisle seat we have left is in first class. Because you've been so patient, we're upgrading your ticket. Come with me, and I'll take you to your seat."

Because the woman was patient, she received favored treatment from the airline employees. If an airline can give someone favored treatment, how much more will God do the same for those he loves! The fourth key to keeping an alliance with God is to realize that God's favor never fails. Remember, favor means goodwill; approval; to prefer or help, do a kindness for or endorse. When we are favored, we are regarded or treated favorably, are provided with advantages, or are especially privileged. God's favor is a very special kind of favor: it's a promise you can rely on, especially when you've been faithful in the midst of life's storms.

Notice how God poured out his favor on Paul. God didn't just set him up in a hut. The Bible tells us that God prepared an estate for him; and it wasn't just any estate—it was the private villa of the chief Roman official on the island. It was as if God had turned an island in the middle of nowhere into Club Med. Now that's favor!

To make things even better, God's favor extended beyond the generosity of Publius to that of the islanders, who honored Paul and the shipwrecked crew in many ways. In fact, when they were ready to sail again, the people of Malta furnished them with the supplies they needed.[25] God's favor even extended to the provision of a ship on which Paul and his men were able to continue their voyage to Rome.

Imagine what those who greeted Paul in Rome thought when they saw that Alexandrian ship pulling into the harbor. They must have thought Paul had enjoyed a blissful journey to Rome in the prime sailing season, rather than the nearly disastrous one God had brought him through. As for Paul, I think he must have been content and grateful, thanking God for his divine favor.

Because of his unwavering faith and unfaltering alliance with God, and because he was blessed with God's favor, Paul fulfilled his divinely appointed mission to Rome. For two years he stayed there in his own rented house, welcoming and teaching all who came to see him. Although still a prisoner, Paul preached the kingdom of God and taught about the Lord Jesus Christ boldly and without hindrance.[26] He unashamedly enjoyed the favor of God that never fails.

God's favor does for us what a baby does for a mother who holds her child for the first time after a painful delivery—he makes us forget all about the painful process and leads us to gratefully acknowledge that it was all worth it.

God wants his never-ending favor to help you write positive endings to your storm stories. We must never quit on God. If we make and sustain an alliance with God by holding fast to his Word, recognizing that he turns delays into divine appointments, and re-alizing that his favor never fails, he will help us to survive and thrive in the midst of any storm. As Paul discovered, no matter what a storm's cause, God can use it to turn our lives around and give us a new direction.

9

CELEBRATING THE WAYS GOD
MADE YOU SPECIAL

At the beginning of this book, I told you about a time when my life needed a turnaround. I had suffered from sleepless nights on and off for about three months because of the stress of both personal and church-related concerns. I cried out to God night after night, but it seemed to me as though he were ignoring my pleas for help. Looking back now, though, I can see that I was wrong. God wasn't ignoring my cries, nor was he disinterested in my turmoil. Instead, he was orchestrating my turnaround to give me a new direction better than anything I had dreamed.

I still have occasional sleepless nights, of course, brought on by the kinds of struggles we all experience, but God caused all those things I was going through to work together for good. He used my time of struggle to help me understand that he can rescue any of us and give us new direction. He gave me the seven circumstances that make up the central chapters in this book and showed me how he works each of them for our good. Then he guided me to write the words you've been reading—words that I hope will inspire and provide encouragement to others who may need a turnaround.

At first, because this is what pastors do, all I did was use those seven circumstances as the basis for a sermon series. The day after the first sermon, about how God can turn our lives around when we're headed down the wrong road, something happened that proved to be the first step in God's turnaround of my own life. My literary agent and I attended a meeting at a publishing firm for Christian books in New York. After opening pleasantries, the publisher revealed that he had been at my church the previous Sunday. "I must tell you that it was a defining moment in my life," he said. "The message you gave spoke strongly to me and really challenged me to begin to draw closer to God. As a matter of fact, I believe you ought to turn it into the first book that we hope you will write for us."

Although I didn't end up signing a contract with that particular publishing house, the experience made me realize that God had, indeed, heard every prayer I'd prayed. All along, he was divinely orchestrating a plan to work all things together for good in my life.

God's favor to me extended even further, in a most unexpected way. I had formed the habit, during my troubled prayers, of journaling my thoughts—writing them down in much the same way David did in his psalms. And, as David's often did, sometimes my worshipful musings took the form of song lyrics, as though I were singing to the Lord. It occurred to me that the songs in my mind actually sounded like real music. So I continued to write them down, and as I did, I began to hear melodies in my head that seemed to go with the words. That may not be much of a miracle for a musically talented person, but it certainly was a miracle for me. Even my devoted wife cringes when she hears me humming or singing. She insists I'm tone deaf. So I'm not sure that even God would consider my singing a joyful noise.

Despite my lack of musical ability, I wrote down the songs and remembered the melodies—but without the slightest thought that they would ever amount to more than just my psalms to God in troubled times.

Then one day I was having lunch with a good friend who happens to be an accomplished songwriter and artist, and I went out on a limb and asked if I could read him some of my lyrics. Although he seemed taken aback and doubtful, he indulged me. I'll never forget that day. As I read the lyrics of the first few songs to him, tears formed in his eyes, right there in the steakhouse.

"You wrote those songs?" he asked in obvious surprise. When I confirmed that I had, he told me that he'd just returned from a songwriters' conference where he had offered to help any new songwriter to find a publisher if the young composer could write a song on the spot that could move him. He added that no one there had managed to do so but that I just had.

I was flabbergasted—a Dove Award–winning composer was offering to help me with my music! Since then I've written eighty-five songs, with the music already composed for about fifteen of them, and I'm getting ready to record a demo album. Five of the songs have already been sung in my church, and when I hear our congregation worshipping God in response to them, I'm overcome with joy and gratitude. Talk about a new direction for my life: I'm a tone-deaf wonder writing songs others actually enjoy.

When I think about it, I'm in awe of all God has done for me—of how he took my pain, my heartache, my trials, and my tests, and like a skillful tapestry maker, he wove them together for good. He truly can turn our lives around, a fact to which the original lyrics (since modified) of one of the first songs God placed in my mind bears testimony. Born during those sleepless nights, the song is called "Tapestry Maker":

> *I declare you Tapestry Maker,*
> *Molder and Shaper,*
> *Lord of my mess,*
> *King of distress,*
> *Taking the pieces and making for me*
> *Not just a painting but a tapestry.*

How did I learn that?
What did that mean?
How came that to happen?
What can this be?

Was it by chance or could it be meant?
Is it a problem or part of your plan?
Give me your thoughts and help me to see
That you are weaving my tapestry.

So I declare you Tapestry Maker,
Molder and Shaper,
Lord of my mess,
King of distress,
Taking the pieces and making for me
Not just a painting but a tapestry.

How you do it I'll never know.
Weaving joy from sorrow is a feat beyond my ken.
But in your hands miracles are made,
Weaving together a life that won't fade.
So I declare you Tapestry Maker,
Molder and Shaper,
Lord of my mess,
King of distress,
Taking the pieces and making for me
Not just a painting but a tapestry.

From shattered pieces and parts that don't fit,
You put all together, and now I see
That what seemed unlinked
Was part of your plan,
Weaving a tapestry with your hand.

So I declare you Tapestry Maker,
Molder and Shaper,
Lord of my mess,
King of distress,
Taking the pieces and making for me
Not just a painting but a tapestry.

The gift of writing these songs was only a part of how God worked all things together for my good when I needed a life turnaround. Looking back now, I wouldn't trade those sleepless nights for restful ones, because I now understand that God can turn our lives around when we're headed down the wrong road. He can turn our lives around when we've blown it. He can turn our lives around when no one believes in us. He can turn our lives around when we've walked away from him. He can turn our lives around when things are out of our control. He can turn our lives around when we're trapped. And he can turn our lives around when we find ourselves in a storm. How do I know that God can turn our lives around? I know it because he did it for me; and if he did it for me, I know that he can do it for you!

Just as important as knowing that God can turn our lives around, however, is knowing that God *wants* to do so. And the reason he wants to turn our lives around is because you and I are special to him.

Since life's tribulations can sometimes make us forget or even doubt how special we are in God's eyes, we need to fix that precious truth in our hearts as an axiom of faith. Coming to understand that we are special begins with the realization of where we came from. The word *special* means extraordinary, unique, and exceptional; and that's exactly what each of us is. You and I are the pinnacle of God's creation. Everything God created was good; but after he created mankind, he added an adverb to intensify the adjective that describes his creation. He said that it was *very* good.[1]

What is it about us that makes us special? The answer is that we were not patterned after monkeys, chimpanzees, or gorillas but after God himself. We find that truth in the first chapter of Genesis: "God said, 'Let us make human beings in our image, to be like us.' "² That is what makes us special, and it's a truth almost too wonderful to comprehend.

We often hear children talking about whom they wish they could grow up to be like. They say things like, "When I grow up, I want to be like LeBron James," or "When I grow up, I want to be like Tiger Woods." Those are good aspirations, but they fall far short of the truth that you and I were created to be like God!

Scripture affirms that truth over and over, as in the eighth Psalm: "What are mere mortals that you should think about them, human beings that you should care for them? Yet you made them only a little lower than God and crowned them with glory and honor. You gave them charge of everything you made, putting all things under their authority."³ Those are astounding statements that speak to one amazing truth—that we are special because we are like God!

From the beginning of time, the enemy of our souls has tried to blind us to the fact that we are special because we are like God. After God created the first man and woman and placed them in a paradise where good ruled over evil, the devil came along and caused mankind and all creation to fall by challenging Adam and Eve's likeness to God.

The serpent was more crafty than any of the wild animals the LORD God had made. He said to the woman, "Did God really say, 'You must not eat from any tree in the garden'?"

The woman said to the serpent, "We may eat fruit from the trees in the garden, but God did say, 'You must not eat fruit from the tree that is in the middle of the garden, and you must not touch it, or you will die.' "

"You will not surely die," the serpent said to the woman. "For

God knows that when you eat of it your eyes will be opened, and you will be like God, knowing good and evil."

When the woman saw that the fruit of the tree was good for food and pleasing to the eye, and also desirable for gaining wisdom, she took some and ate it. She also gave some to her husband, who was with her, and he ate it.[4]

What a deception! Adam and Eve were already like God. They didn't have to eat an apple to become Godlike. The sad futility of it all becomes evident, of course, when we come to understand that the significance we seek was already provided to us by God in the beginning, when he made us and told us we are like him!

We haven't learned our lesson, though. The enemy of our souls still has us convinced that we are anything other than created in the image and likeness of God. We are particularly susceptible to believing that lie when we're headed down the wrong road, when we've blown it, when no one believes in us, when we've walked away from God, when things seem out of control, when we're trapped, or when life's storms strike. At those times we question our value. We wonder why God would want to bother turning our lives around. And we're likely to feel anything but special.

We are special, though, particularly in God's eyes. He has created each of us with seven God-like characteristics that make us SPECIAL. We must keep these in mind so that we will always remember and trust that, in every one of those situations listed above, God wants to turn our lives around.

Self-Direction

We're special because we alone, of all God's creation, have the power of self-direction. Have you ever wondered why the world sometimes seems to be spinning out of control? Sickness, disease, tsunamis, hurricanes, and wars seem to be on the rise. It almost seems as if God has turned his back on us. That may be the reason many people choose to ignore God and refuse to place their faith in him. Before falling into that error, though, we need to take a closer look.

When God first created the world and mankind, he had nothing but good in mind. As Gregg Wear points out in his book *Beating the Blame Game*, God originally made the world perfect. The food grew in the soil without fail: there were no weeds, thorns, or blight to damage crops. The land teemed with life, as did the water and skies. No pollution or disease or dangerous animals threatened mankind. Adam and Eve had nothing to fear—not even death. "The earth was truly the paradise that God envisioned it to be. No dangerous jungle. No over soaked, deadly swamp. No barren desert."[5] The earth was like what we now imagine heaven to be like. Life was a pulsating, vibrant force. No sickness, no disease, no death. The earth was a dynamic, aesthetically beautiful, and tranquil place made not by happenstance but by design—a design in anticipation of God's crowning creation. God designed the world for you and me.

And he created the earth as a Father who was about to create a family. The Scriptures tell us that God created the world to be inhabited.[6] We were not made as an afterthought. Humanity is not some cosmic accident. God made human beings on purpose, as the culmination of a great plan that he conceived and carried out according to his own pleasure. God is the ultimate Father who went to great lengths to establish a perfect environment for his children.

The only missing element in the perfect environment was the ability of God's creation—us—to love him back. So our Father set out to create an environment where true love could exist. But this decision carried with it a risk, because it involved giving individuals free will—the ability to be self-directed.

As an illustration, imagine a marriage where every day, three

(178)

times a day, the man asks his wife if she loves him, and her response is always the same: "Yes, dear, I love you with all my heart." With that in mind, one might conclude that the marriage is founded on true love.

Let's add the detail, however, that the woman tells her husband that she loves him with all her heart only because he brutally beats her if she gives him any other response. In other words, he forces her to say what he wants to hear.

Knowing that, we can see that the marriage is not based on true love. Instead, it's built on conditioned responses prompted by fear. For true love to exist, there must be free will—the ability to choose to give or withhold one's affection.

This illustration is revealing when we apply it to God's relationship with humanity. He could have created us programmed to love, serve, and obey him. He could have exercised his power over us to force us to submit to him. But doing either would have run contrary to creating an environment of true love. So instead he chose to give us free will—the ability to choose for ourselves—even though it was all but guaranteed that at least some people would make bad choices that would result in adverse consequences. For example, the gift of free will made it possible for our first ancestors to disobey God and partake of the fruit of the tree of the knowledge of good and evil, a choice with the direst of consequences: expulsion from paradise and eventual death.

But God didn't entirely abandon us to the consequences of our bad choices. He didn't leave us high and dry, as some have chosen to believe. Rather, he did something extraordinary that we'll explore in the next section. For now, we need only understand that self-direction makes us special, distinguishing us from the rest of God's creation and making us like God. God loved us so much that he chose to keep his power in check by granting us power to choose to accept or reject him—the ability that perhaps makes us more like God than does any other attribute he has given us.

Power

The second Godlike attribute that makes us special is power itself. The story of creation makes God's power obvious; but the power God has given to man needs further explanation.

Genesis tells us that as God contemplated his greatest creation, he said, "Let Us make man in Our image, according to Our likeness; let them have dominion [or power] over the fish of the sea, over the birds of the air, and over the cattle, over all the earth and over every creeping thing that creeps on the earth."[7] It is clear, therefore, that God provided each of us with power—power that we can use to hurt or heal, to build or destroy, to encourage or disparage, to reach out or reject, to do good or evil. History is replete with tyrants, such as Hitler, Stalin, and Saddam Hussein, who use their power to do evil. We are perhaps most like God, however, when we use our power to do good.

Jesus knew that and admonished us with a simple bit of advice often referred to as the Golden Rule. He told us to ask ourselves what we want people to do for us and then take the initiative to do if for them.[8] We might even think of that advice from Jesus—a highpoint of the greatest sermon ever preached, the Sermon on the Mount—as the most important point in a CliffsNotes-type summary of the Bible's message about relating to others.

Most of us are familiar with the Golden Rule, of course, and some of us have even come up with our own revised versions of it: do unto others *before* they do unto you; do unto others *after* they've done it to you; and do unto others one better than they've done to you. One little girl, confused about the exact meaning of the famous rule, wrote a letter to God, asking for clarification. "Dear God," she wrote, "Did you really mean 'Do unto others as they do unto you'? Because if you did, I'm really gonna fix my brother!"

Whatever version of the Golden Rule you may have heard or devised for yourself, one thing is certain: it presupposes one of the greatest of truths—that you and I have the power to do good to others. And that beneficial use of our God-given power makes us very much like him.

Many years ago a couple took their sick child to the New Jersey coast, hoping the sea air would improve the child's health. When they arrived at the seashore, all of the hotels were booked. At one small lodging, however, the manager refused to turn the family away. He and his wife gave their own rooms to the couple and their sick child. The child recovered, and the family left, promising to reward the manager for his kindness.

Several years later, after the manager had moved to a hotel in Philadelphia, he received an invitation from the millionaire William Waldorf Astor to visit New York City. Astor took the surprised manager on a tour of a luxurious new hotel on the corner of Fifth Avenue and Thirty-Fourth Street in Manhattan—and then offered him the job of running it, revealing that the family for whom the manager had given up his rooms years earlier were relatives of Mr. Astor. The couple had lobbied Astor to build the hotel, all along planning for it to be the reward they had promised. George C. Boldt accepted the opportunity, becoming the manager and president of the Waldorf-Astoria Hotel, a position that eventually made him a millionaire in his own right.[9]

The manager chose to use his power to do good and learned that doing so benefits not only the receiver of a good deed but also the doer.

Jesus chose to use his power for good. He could have remained in heaven and continued ruling the heavens and the earth, but instead, he used his power to come to earth and die on a cross for the sins of mankind.

What you and I do with our power is up to us, but by putting our energies into doing good, we are following Jesus' example and acting as God would act.

Excellence

We have the power to be excellent in every way. As we've already seen, until God created Adam and Eve, God had called all of his creations simply "good." But he described his creation of mankind as "very good,"[10] suggesting that among all of his works, we are something special. The New Living Translation of the Bible gives us a new insight when it tells us, "God looked over all he had made, and he saw that it was excellent in every way."[11] And that, of course, entitles humanity to a third special characteristic—that we, too, are excellent in every way.

Have you ever wondered why you are the way you are? Why you have the personality you have? Why you possess a particular assortment of gifts? Why you have particular likes and dislikes? Why you have the physical and intellectual characteristics that distinguish you from others? Most of us have wondered about those things at some point. Sadly, many of us have been disappointed with ourselves, wishing that we were different instead of rejoicing in the person God created us to be.

God wants us to know that we're the way we are for specific reasons. He designed all of us to accomplish the specific purposes he intends for us as individuals. That means that we are all perfectly suited for whatever those purposes might be. Even our "warts" and shortcomings are beautiful to God. The following story illustrates how even those things we think are the worst about ourselves can be used as part of God's design.

It was midsummer 1969, and Dave Roever sweated in the jungle heat on a gunboat in Vietnam. Handsome and recently married, Dave only wanted to finish his tour of duty and return home to his bride, whom he hadn't seen for eight months. But on this day, the Navy gunner's mate had a mission to scout out the enemy's strength along a river.

The shores were covered with brush, and the crew of the small gunboat couldn't see beyond the edge of the water. Roever threw an incendiary grenade to burn aside the undergrowth. After the grenade ignited, Roever noticed movement and pulled out a second grenade. As he prepared to throw it, it exploded in his hand. The white-hot phosphorous covered his upper body, from his head to his waist, and he toppled off the boat into the river.

By the time a fellow crewman found Dave where he had swum to shore, he was so badly burned that he was presumed dead. Even the medics who saw him after he was flown to Saigon thought Roever was only a blackened corpse; focusing on other patients, they didn't attempt to neutralize the phosphorous, which continued to burn Roever's body. When Dave mustered the strength to call out to them, they were shocked into action. The blackened corpse was alive!

Days later, in a hospital in Japan, Dave asked for a mirror. A doctor tried to dissuade him, but the young man insisted. He wanted to see what had happened. The face Roever saw, he did not recognize as his own. He was hideously scarred. His right eye was blind; his right ear was burned away, along with most of his nose. He was also missing parts of his right hand where the grenade had exploded. The once handsome young man now looked like a monster.

Despairing, that night Dave pulled out one of his IVs, assuming that without medicine, he would die. But he only woke up hungry. When a local missionary who knew Dave came to pray for him, Dave realized he didn't want to die. He decided to trust that God would bring about good in his life.

Flown home at last to Santa Barbara, California, Dave didn't know what his wife would think. But when she came into the hospital room for the first time, she bent over his charred face, kissed him tenderly, and whispered, "I just want you to know, I love you."

Despite extensive reconstructive surgery, Dave Roever's face and hands still bear the scars of his ordeal. But instead of hiding or bemoaning his fate, Dave has turned his marred visage into a blessing. Today he's a popular speaker, visiting schools, churches, veterans' organizations, and military bases. He uses his story and his face to share God's power to make the most of any life. He also operates an innovative program that takes Vietnam veterans and their families on humanitarian trips to Vietnam so they can deal with the wounds of their own pasts as they take medicine, clothing, and other necessities to the poor in that nation. They focus on Vietnamese children who have suffered deformities due to accidents or birth defects caused by lingering chemical pollutants from the war. Dave's ability to smile and laugh despite his own appearance lifts the spirits of these children, teaching them that they, too, can rejoice in who they are.

Dave Roever came to accept that even after life had scarred him, God had still made him excellent in every way. His disfigured face, a "thumb" made out of a fold of skin from his hip (Dave calls it a "thip")—the very things we would expect him to most want to change—Dave has learned to treasure and use for God's glory. Dave has gone beyond merely accepting these differences to celebrating them as part of God's plan for his life![12]

Remember Fanny Crosby and her attitude about being blind? She looked upon her blindness as a gift. Remember one-handed football players Trey Woods and DaWuan Miller? They never saw themselves as handicapped. Indeed, Miller learned that his bony, clublike arm was a defensive advantage when school-yard bullies picked fights[13] (it probably was pretty effective for hitting wide receivers too).

The next time you find yourself wishing that God had made you differently or that you had someone else's gifts, stop and reflect for a moment. God made you for a purpose. You, and no one else, are uniquely qualified—uniquely designed—for that purpose. If you were different, you could not fulfill that purpose. You would not even be you. Instead of complaining about your flaws, start considering them as unique qualifications. Pay attention to the ways God is already using them in your life, even without your knowing it.

When Dave Roever was injured by the grenade, a fellow sailor took one look at Roever's burned body and his continued declaration of faith in God and accepted Christ on the spot. God used Roever's deformity and his reaction to it the instant it happened! If God can do that for Dave, what can he do with your differences? Maybe you'll discover, like the popular Christmas reindeer with the glowing nose, that the one thing that sets you apart and that you like least about yourself is the one thing those around you truly need!

You are the way you are because God has a special plan for your life. He designed you to be excellent in every way, even the parts you might like to change. You never know whether the very thing you see as your greatest weakness may just be what God uses most.

Creative Potential

We're special not only because of our God-given attributes of self-direction, power, and excellence, but also because of our creative potential. Have you ever found yourself amazed by the creative genius of mankind?

- Thomas Edison invented the phonograph and the incandescent light bulb.
- Alexander Graham Bell invented the telephone.
- German scientist Karl Braun invented the cathode ray tube that for many years served as the picture tube in televisions and still has myriad technological uses.
- Wilbur and Orville Wright pioneered the powered airplane, which they patented as a "flying machine."

- Henry Ford conceived and introduced the Model T automobile that heralded the beginning of the Motor Age.
- Sir Alexander Fleming discovered penicillin, an antibiotic that has saved countless lives.

The list of humanity's creative achievements is virtually endless!

Of course, no real quantitative parallel can be drawn between mankind's creative potential and the limitless creative power of God so impressively chronicled in the book of Genesis. Nevertheless, mankind's God-given creative ability is undeniable, and its potential is in all of us from before the time we can even walk or talk.

One of my good friends has an eight-year-old son, Wesley. His affection for me probably has something to do with the bucket of tokens I gave him so he could play the games in our church arcade and ride in one of the toy cars. He'd put in the tokens, and off he would go, with the car rocking and jerking to music.

Later, Wesley amazed me by creating a tiny replica of the car ride out of tape and paper—an astonishing creative accomplishment illustrative of one of the many ways in which God has made us like him.

Our creative ability makes us feel good too. The smile of accomplishment on Wesley's face when he handed me his miniature masterpiece reminded me of the same look of satisfaction I used to see on my father's face after he had finished mowing the lawn, painting a room, or rebuilding his 1978 Ford Pinto. Feelings of accomplishment are, in their own way, not unlike the pleasure that God, the source of our creative ability, must have felt when he looked over all that he had created and pronounced it "very good."[14]

So the next time you're victimized by the misguided notion that God wouldn't want to turn your life around, reflect on your own creative accomplishments—the meal you just made for your family, the room you just designed, the strategic plan you spearheaded at work—even the outfit you pulled together for that party last week. The sense of achievement you feel from those creative acts is a reminder of one significant way that God has made you special.

Imagination

Our creative potential is often activated by the fifth characteristic God has built into each of us to make us special—imagination. Unfortunately, organized religion has frowned upon that wonderful gift for so long that many people of faith have suppressed their imaginations. Having been led to believe that using the imagination often leads to the pursuit of carnal pleasures, many people have underrated or questioned that God-given gift.

But what if God had never allowed himself to imagine? The answer is that you and I would never have been born. Purpose motivated God to create us, but it was God's imagination that gave form to his creation.

Imagination always precedes creation. To create, we must first formulate a design in our mind's eye. Years ago a successful man in Hollywood, named Arthur, got a call from his friend Walter, inviting him along on a trip to see an investment property. Walter was a good guy, successful in his own right, but his imagination could be a little grand. Still, Arthur decided to go along. After about an hour's drive "into the sticks," the car stopped. "Here it is!" Walter announced.

Arthur looked around and saw nothing but a big field of dirt and a few bulldozers. But his friend began to describe the grand resort he planned to build, full of places to eat, stores, shows, and elaborate carnival rides. Then he suggested that Arthur buy up the property around his own, promising that when the resort was finished, the land would be in demand for hotels and other commercial use, easily worth twenty times what Arthur might pay if he invested early. Arthur looked at his friend and thought he was nuts. Old Walt had really gone over the edge on this one. A resort with kiddie rides in the middle of nowhere, miles from the happening places of Hollywood and L.A.? He smiled and politely declined the offer.

That's how Art Linkletter rejected his friend Walt Disney's advice and missed investing in the creation of Disneyland. Walter's grand imagination had seen something Arthur could not.[15] Where Art Linkletter had seen only dirt and the inconvenience of a long drive, Walt Disney saw the Magic Kingdom fully built and filled with happy families from around the world. Before it was constructed, Walt conceived the design of Disneyland in his imagination, and his vision spawned its creation. Imagination always precedes creation. We can never create what we don't first imagine.

Our imagination is a transporter of sorts, not unlike the "transporter" in *Star Trek* that Captain Kirk would famously ask chief engineer Scott to use when he clicked open his communicator and said, "Beam me up, Scotty." Scotty would then activate the transporter, which would beam up any member of the *Enterprise* crew from anywhere on the planet back to the mother ship. The transporter worked by dematerializing people or things in one place and rematerializing them almost instantaneously in another.

Our imagination is a little like a transporter. That God-given faculty, when used in accordance with God's instructions, brings the invisible things seen only in our mind's eye into the material world. Our imaginations materialize our dreams.

The nineteenth-century proverb I shared with you in chapter five describes that process: "Sow a thought, and you reap an act." Our minds were made to figure out ways to accomplish what they imagine. When we set about imagining something, our minds become creative and begin to give us ideas for realizing that vision.

First comes thought, then organizing ideas and plans to actualize that thought, and finally the materialization of those ideas and plans as reality. So if anyone tries to thwart your gift of imagination, remember that all things are created twice: first in our imagination and then for the world to see.

The power of imagination to inspire our Godlike creativity is beautifully illustrated by the life of Michelangelo. You recall the story about Michelangelo's creating his statue *David* out of a broken slab of marble? Throughout his life, the artist would explain the process he used to produce that masterpiece, as well as all of his other sculptures. He believed that the statue, when conceived by the artist, existed within the marble. It was the artist's task to release it by chipping away the superfluous stone. So when Michelangelo picked up his stools, he believed his imagination had already created the statue; with his hammer and chisel, he was simply removing the stone that covered it.[16]

Take a moment to look around you. If you're sitting in chair, notice the chair. If you're indoors, notice the walls around you. Notice the doors, the windows, the clothing you wear. Feel the weight of this book. Notice the ink, the paper, the typeface—even the letters. Nothing that you see would exist had not some person— someone just like you or me—used God's gift of imagination to see it and create it. Just like the God who made us, we are all creators, imagining the world we want and acting to bring it about. The power of imagination is in each of us, and God's desire is for you to use it to his great glory and your great good.

Acceptance

We all know how important it is to be accepted. When people accept us, it makes us feel valuable; it lifts our spirits and motivates us. And just as others can lift us up by accepting us, we have the power to offer this gift to others. Acceptance means valuing others just as they are. It means respecting their ideas because we respect them. It means allowing them to talk about how they feel inside, and why they feel that way, without fear of rejection. Acceptance doesn't mean that we can never help people understand when they're wrong; but it does mean that we allow them to feel safe about expressing themselves freely. In short, acceptance simply makes others feel free to be themselves, even if we don't always approve of what they say or do. We respect others as they are.

God allowed Adam and Eve to enjoy the gift of acceptance even after they had sinned. In the third chapter of Genesis, we read that when God visited Adam and Eve in the garden after they had disobeyed him, exercising their self-direction wrongly, he still called out to them. When they heard God's voice, they hid, knowing full well that they had done wrong.

Being God, of course, the Creator was fully aware of what Adam and Eve had done. Yet he asked them rhetorically where they were, and Adam replied, "I heard you in the garden, and I was afraid because I was naked; so I hid."[17] God then expressed his displeasure over their choice to sin and told them about the consequences that would ensue. In his compassionate understanding of the distress they were feeling because of their newly acquired knowledge of good and evil, however, he covered their nakedness with animal skins and offered them the gift of acceptance. He didn't condone their sin, nor did he exempt them from its consequences; but he did love them even as they were. It was God's gift of acceptance that made possible mankind's eventual redemption and reconciliation.[18]

Jesus also offered the gift of acceptance to many with whom he came in contact as he walked the earth. One such instance can be found in Luke 7:36–50. The setting was a dinner party in the home of Simon, a Pharisee. Here's the scene as I imagine it: Simon invited Jesus for dinner, along with many of the movers and shakers of Jesus' time; Jesus, contrary to popular expectation, accepted the invitation. All the preparations had been carefully planned and executed, and a doorman had been stationed at the door to ensure that only those on the A list were allowed in.

The dinner party was going perfectly, with everyone partaking of the elaborate hors d'oeuvres, when an uninvited but well-known visitor appeared on the scene—well-known not because of her contributions to society but because of her sinful behavior. She made a beeline for Jesus: "As she stood behind him at his feet weeping, she began to wet his feet with her tears. Then she wiped them with her hair, kissed them and poured perfume on them."[19]

Simon obviously disapproved—not just of the woman's sin but of Jesus himself. He thought: "If this man were a prophet, he would know who is touching him and what kind of woman she is—that she is a sinner."[20]

The choice confronting Jesus was obvious: he could either reject the woman because of her sin and gain the favor of the host and dinner guests, or accept her and earn their scorn. Jesus chose the latter. He offered the undeserving woman the gift of acceptance.

Like God the Father, Jesus sees people differently than you and I do. We often judge others externally, but God sees past our tattered exteriors to the potential in each of us. Perhaps you, like Jesus, are a vehicle that God wants to use to release the beauty hidden deep within someone he sees as special.

Love

The last of the seven Godlike characteristics that make us special is the power we possess to love the unlovable. As we shall see, this is possibly our greatest Godlike attribute. Yet it seems at odds with the realities of the world as we know it, where love is usually perceived as either deserved or earned, and where any expression of love that falls outside of those boundaries is looked upon as peculiar or even perverse.

For evidence of that, we need look no further than any simple act of kindness shown to a stranger. For example, once when my son and I were with some friends at Shea Stadium, we discovered that our seats were in the top rows; so I decided (because of my aversion to heights) to try to exchange the tickets for seats closer to the field. Although I wasn't able to make an exchange, I was able to obtain additional lodge-level seats; so I decided to give the tickets for the upper-level seats that we had originally been assigned to a group of young people. They were not only grateful but surprised by my apparent generosity.

One of my friends, also surprised by my action, asked why I had given the tickets to the kids, and I replied that I had done it to bless them. When he then reminded me that the tickets had already been scanned when we originally entered the stadium and that they would be rejected when presented a second time, I realized that my intended good deed would ultimately only reinforce the erroneous notion in the minds of those suspicious young people that unmerited love or kindness doesn't really exist.

Some love, however, truly does operate on a higher level—God's system of love. This philosophy of love is succinctly described in one powerful bit of Scripture: "Love your enemies! Do good to them. Lend to them without expecting to be repaid. Then your reward from heaven will be very great, and you will truly be acting as children of the Most High, for he is kind to those who are unthankful and wicked."[21] Notice that God's system of love is quite different from ours, since it is in no way based on apparent merit.

God's system of love is the agape-love system. *Agape* is one of the Greek words for love used in the New Testament. It stands in stark contrast to our earned-love system because it is a conscious choice of the mind instead of a response of the heart. Rather than a system of love based on payback or instinctive emotion, *agape* is a fundamental rule of behavior toward others that guides our actions—in other words, *agape* means that we *choose* to love. We love because we will to do so.

Think about it. Are you going to love your enemies by accident? Of course not! No one just "happens" to love an enemy. It's against our normal instincts. When someone hurts us or frightens us, we want to defend ourselves. We either want to lash out and attack, find a way to block off the danger, or even hide from it. In order for us to love our enemies, we must control our instincts and emotions. Agape is an intentional discipline that guides our actions. It is a supreme expression of our first Godlike attribute—our self-direction. Agape makes us able to love the unlovable and undeserving.[22]

Notice that in the scripture quoted above, we are told that when we love like that, we are acting like God. In another passage, Jesus explained God's unconditional love by stating that "he causes his sun to rise on the evil and the good, and sends rain on the righteous and the unrighteous."[23] Here in the lush green New World of America, we often misread this passage, thinking the rain alludes to bad times. After all, rain interrupts our baseball games! But in the dry lands of the Middle East, where water is scarce, rain is always a blessing. Jesus was declaring that no matter what we do or how we think, God's greatest desire is to bless us. Agape is heavenly love, motivated not by emotion or hope of repayment but by a conscious desire to do good toward others.

The most amazing attribute of that heavenly love is its power to change people for the better. This is illustrated by the story of Norma McCorvey, better known to most of us as the "Jane Roe" in the Supreme Court's 1973 *Roe v. Wade* decision. The national headquarters for Operation Rescue (now Operation Save America) had moved into offices beside the abortion clinic where McCorvey worked. When word got out that Flip Benham, the national director of Operation Rescue, had privately sought her out, everyone expected to hear about an angry confrontation. But instead, Benham had come to McCorvey to apologize. When he had met her the year before, Benham had accused her of causing the deaths of millions of babies, laying the abortion crisis at her feet. Benham told her he knew immediately that his words had hurt her and that he regretted them. He asked her to forgive him. McCorvey admitted the words had indeed hurt, and she accepted his apology.

Surprising everyone, McCorvey and Benham developed a friendship. As Benham and his fellow workers at Operation Rescue showed unconditional love and support to McCorvey, she began to realize that the abortion workers around her cared only for her status as a national symbol. She was merely a rallying cry in their eyes, not a person with feelings. Her concerns or questions about what they were doing were brushed aside in favor of a political agenda. She increasingly came to appreciate the kindness of Benham and the others at Operation Rescue, surprised that these people, whom the pro-choice movement called "terrorists," always responded to her with love.

The most persistent source of love was a young girl named Emily, the daughter of an Operation Rescue volunteer. Emily repeatedly invited Norma to church, but Norma, who put her faith in a mishmash of crystals, runes, and tarot cards, always made excuses. Finally, one summer Sunday, Norma gave in and agreed to attend the service with her young friend's family. That day she accepted Christ. The news stunned the world, and to everyone's further astonishment, the person Norma requested to baptize her was Flip Benham. Today Norma McCorvey proudly proclaims her faith in Christ and has started her own ministry in opposition to abortion—in particular, in support of Crisis Pregnancy Centers. "The pro-choice movement is more concerned about its cause and the mythical Jane Roe," Benham later wrote, "but our God is concerned about the person of Norma McCorvey."[24]

McCorvey's conversion reminds all of us of the power of unconditional love to change people for the better. You and I also have that power. The apostle Paul told us that love is the greatest gift of all.[25] John told us "God is love."[26] We receive our power to love from God—and nothing could make us more special.

So there we are. These seven simple, Godlike, God-given characteristics remind us that we are special. We have the power of self-direction. We have the power of power itself. We have the power to be excellent in every way. We have the power of creative potential. We have the power to imagine. We have the power to offer others the gift of acceptance. And we have the power to love the unlovable. Those seven extraordinary traits all point to one irrefutable conclusion: we are special in God's eyes and worth redeeming, even when . . .

- we're headed down the wrong road.
- we've blown it.
- no one believes in us.
- we've walked away from God.
- we're out of control.
- we're trapped, and
- we're going through a storm.

God wants to turn our lives around. He's always ready to give us a new direction—the perfect direction for the life he's had designed for us all along.

ACKNOWLEDGMENTS

Nobel Peace Prize recipient Elie Wiesel once wrote, "There is divine beauty in learning, just as there is human beauty in tolerance. To learn means to accept the postulate that life did not begin at my birth. Others have been here before me, and I walk in their footsteps. The books I have read were composed by generations of fathers and sons, mothers and daughters, teachers and disciples. I am the sum total of their experiences, their quests. And so are you."[1] In writing this book, perhaps more than any other time, I have understood that truth.

So it is with that in mind that I want to express my gratitude to the following wonderful people who have influenced me along the way: my parents, Frank and Fran, for teaching me by example about the true nature of our heavenly Father; my uncle John, for introducing our family to Jesus; my spiritual mentors, Dad Fletcher, Rick Renner, and Anthony Storino, for continuing to bless me with both practical and spiritual truths to enrich my life; my good friend Courtenay Caublé, for monitoring my writing and bringing out the best in me; and of course Denny and Philis Boultinghouse, my editors at Howard Books, for their guidance and many invaluable suggestions.

NOTES

1: LOOKING FOR THE GOOD IN LIFE

1. Max Lucado, *Traveling Light* (Dallas, TX: W Publishing Group, 2001), 45.
2. William F. Braasch, M.D., *Early Days in the Mayo Clinic* (Springfield, IL: Charles C. Thomas, 1969), 15–17. Also see "The Tradition and Heritage of Mayo Clinic," Mayo Foundation for Medical Education and Research, http://www.mayoclinic.org/tradition-heritage/ (accessed June 4, 2009).
3. William Claiborne, "Beethoven: A Life Undone by Heavy Metal?" *Washington Post*, October 18, 2000, A03, http://www.washingtonpost.com/ac2/wp-dyn?pagename=article&node=&contentId=A25895-2000Oct17 (accessed June 11, 2009).
4. David Wyn Jones, *The Life of Beethoven* (Cambridge, UK: Cambridge University Press, 1998), 65–66.
5. Bernard Ruffin, *Fanny Crosby* (n.p.: United Church Press, 1976), 20–21, 26.
6. ChristianHistory.net, "Fanny Crosby," ChristianityToday.com, August 8, 2008, http://www.christianitytoday.com/ch/131christians/poets/crosby.html (accessed June 11, 2009).
7. Ruffin, *Fanny Crosby*, 220.
8. James Stockdale biographical information provided by the official Admiral James Stockdale Web site, http://www.admiralstockdale.com.
9. Jim Collins, *Good to Great* (New York: HarperCollins, 2001), 85.

2: TURNING AROUND WHEN YOU'RE ON THE WRONG ROAD

1. Andy Stanley, *Destinations, Part 1: The Path Principle*, podcast (Alpharetta, GA: North Point Community Church), MP3, http://www.northpoint.org/site/podcasts/ (accessed June 4, 2009).
2. Acts 9:1–5.
3. Acts 9:6.

4. Acts 9:7–9.

5. Acts 22:9.

6. Sir Isaac Newton, Sir Isaac Newton's Mathematical Principles of Natural Philosophy and His System of the World, tr. Andrew Motte, rev. by Florian Cajori (Norwalk, CT: Easton Press, n.d.), 13.

7. Stephen Kinzer, "Bokonbayeva Journal; God of Birds, but Scourge of Foxes and Badgers," *New York Times,* November 4, 1999.

8. 1 Chronicles 4:9 NKJV.

9. 1 Chronicles 4:10 NKJV.

10. 2 Corinthians 12:9.

11. 2 Corinthians 12:10.

12. Dorothy Clarke Wilson, *Ten Fingers for God* (New York: McGraw-Hill, 1965), 144.

13. Wilson, *Ten Fingers,* 144–45.

14. Acts 9:10–12.

15. Acts 9:13–14.

16. Acts 9:17–22.

17. See Acts 4:36–37.

18. Acts 9:5 NKJV.

19. *Merriam-Webster's Collegiate Dictionary,* 11th ed., s.v. "goad."

20. 1 Kings 3:9 MSG.

21. See 1 Kings 3:10–14.

22. Proverbs 3:5–7.

3: MOVING FORWARD AFTER YOU'VE BLOWN IT

1. Dieter Zander, *The Miracle of Mercy,* transcript of sermon delivered April 10, 1996 (South Barrington, IL: Willow Creek Community Church, 1996).

2. Louisa Fletcher, "The Land of Beginning Again," in *The Land of Beginning Again* (Boston: Small, Maynard, 1921), 3.

3. See Philippians 3:13.

4. Traditional fable of India. Retold by Frank Santora and Howard Shirley.

5. See Isaiah 43:25.

6. See Colossians 2:13–14 NLT.

7. See Exodus 1:15–16.

8. See Exodus 2:1–10.

9. Exodus 2:13–14.

10. See Exodus 2:15.

11. This ancient process, known as *cupellation*, is confirmed by the Society of American Silversmiths, http://www.silversmithing.com/silver/faq.

12. The priest is named Reuel in Exodus 2:18, but in all later passages he is referred to as Jethro. Since most people know that name, I have chosen to use it instead.

13. See Exodus 18.

14. Exodus 3:2–4.

15. Jeremiah 31:3–4 NKJV.

16. Jeremiah 29:11.

17. See Romans 8:28.

18. Essie Sakhai, *Persian Rugs and Carpets: The Fabric of Life* (London: Antique Collectors' Club, 2008), 18.

4: REGAINING CONFIDENCE WHEN NO ONE BELIEVES IN YOU

1. Mark 9:23 NKJV.

2. Mark 11:24.

3. *Hoosiers*, directed by David Anspaugh (Orion Pictures, 1986).

4. 1 Samuel 13:14.

5. See 1 Samuel 16:6.

6. See 1 Samuel 16:1–3.

7. See 1 Samuel 16:11.

8. 1 Samuel 16:12–13.

9. Linda Murray, *Michelangelo* (New York: Thames and Hudson, 1980), 38–42.

10. 1 Samuel 16:7.

11. See 1 Samuel 16:14–17.

12. See 1 Samuel 16:18.

13. 1 Samuel 16:23.

14. See 1 Samuel 16:21–22.

15. Jody Goldstein, "With one hand, he's still a terror," *Houston Chronicle*, April 25, 1996.

16. Football Record Book, GoBearKats.com, Sam Houston State University, http://www.gobearkats.com/fls/19900/pdf/records_football.pdf, 11.

17. Tom Friend, "College Football: A Fighter Who Plays Football; Born with No Left Hand, DaWuan Miller Is Boise State Rallying Cry," *New York*

Times, December 7, 1994, http://www.nytimes.com/1994/12/07/sports/
college-football-fighter-who-plays-football-born-with-no-left-hand-
dawuan-miller.html.

18. Football Record Book, 18.
19. Psalm 37:4.
20. 1 Samuel 17:17.
21. Charles R. Swindoll, *Three Steps Forward, Two Steps Back* (Nashville, TN: Thomas Nelson, 1980), 74.
22. Pat Mesiti, *Opportunity Knocks* (Broken Arrow, OK: Dreamhouse, 2001), 5–6.
23. 1 Samuel 17:38–40 NLT.
24. Slings were used in warfare from biblical times well into the Roman era. To this day, visitors to the Middle East can purchase handmade slings of woven flax from local artisans. The general description of slings and their use and character in battle is derived from John Warry, *Warfare in the Classical World* (London: Salamander Books, 1980). Citation is to the Oklahoma Paperbacks edition (1995), throughout, but particularly p. 42.
25. *The Karate Kid*, directed by John G. Alvidsen (Sony Pictures, 1984).
26. 1 Samuel 17:48–51, NLT.
27. Steven L. McKenzie, *King David* (New York: Oxford University Press, 2000), 75.

5: FINDING YOUR WAY BACK WHEN YOU'VE WALKED AWAY
FROM GOD

1. Luke 15:22–24.
2. James 1:13–15.
3. Kenneth E. Bailey, "The Pursuing Father," *Christianity Today*, October 26, 1998.
4. See Deuteronomy 21:17.
5. Kenneth E. Bailey, *Poet and Peasant and Through Peasant Eyes: A Literary-Cultural Approach to the Parables in Luke* (Grand Rapids, MI: Eerdmans, 1983), 161–62.
6. Luke 15:12 NKJV.
7. Catherine Donaldson-Evans, "The Good News of 2005," FoxNews.com, December 30, 2005, http://www.foxnews.com/story/0,2933,180139,00.html (accessed June 8, 2009).
8. Luke 15:17–18 NKJV.

9. Kyle MacDonald, *One Red Paperclip* (New York: Three Rivers, 2007).
10. *Bartlett's Familiar Quotations*, 17th ed. (Boston: Little, Brown, 2002), 849.
11. Bailey, "Pursuing Father."
12. See Deuteronomy 21:18–21.
13. Luke 15:18–19 NKJV.
14. See Isaiah 55:8.
15. Aristotle, quoted in Bailey, *Poet and Peasant*, 181.
16. See Luke 15:22–24.
17. Bailey, "Pursuing Father."
18. See Romans 2:4 NKJV.
19. See Matthew 5:39–44.
20. Matthew 5:45 NKJV.
21. Acts 10:38 NKJV.

6: TRUSTING GOD WHEN LIFE'S OUT OF CONTROL

1. Proverbs 3:5–6.
2. Ron Chernow, *Titan: The Life of John D. Rockefeller, Sr.* (New York: Random House, 1998), 319–23.
3. Robert Kolker, "This Is the Part Where the Superhero Discovers He Is Mortal," *New York,* April 16, 2007, http://nymag.com/news/features/30636/ (accessed June 8, 2009).
4. Associated Press, " 'I'm not a hero,' NYC subway savior says," MSNBC, http://www.msnbc.msn.com/id/16469039/ (accessed June 10, 2009).
5. Kolker, "Superhero Discovers He Is Mortal."
6. The details of this event and Xerxes' plans are told in Herodotus, *The Histories,* trans. Aubrey de Sélincourt, rev. by John Marincola (New York: Penguin, 1996), 373–79.
7. Esther 1:12.
8. Esther 2:17–18.
9. Psalm 139:14–16 MSG.
10. Xerxes' income: Herodotus, *Histories*, 193.
11. Esther 4:11 NLT.
12. Esther 4:13–14.
13. Esther 5:1–2.
14. Psalm 5:12 NKJV.
15. Psalm 30:5.
16. Psalm 84:11.

17. Psalm 145:16 MSG.
18. 2 Corinthians 6:2.
19. 1 Corinthians 15:10 NLT.
20. Esther 5:3.
21. Jeremiah 1:5.
22. Acts 17:25.

7: FREEING YOURSELF WHEN YOU FEEL TRAPPED

1. Genesis 1:1–3.
2. Hebrews 11:1–3 NKJV.
3. Thomas Bullfinch, *Bullfinch's Mythology* (New York: Avenel, 1979), 14–15.
4. Hebrews 11:3 AMP.
5. Hebrews 10:23 KJV.
6. Genesis 17:5.
7. Genesis 17:16.
8. See Proverbs 6:2.
9. Matthew 12:36–37 NKJV.
10. Isaiah 46:10 KJV.
11. See Genesis 12.
12. Luke 8:52–55.
13. John 11:11.
14. John 11:14–15.
15. See Ephesians 5:1.
16. 1 Samuel 17:45–47 NKJV.
17. See Joshua 1:8.
18. See Leviticus 15:19–29.
19. Matthew 9:21 NKJV.
20. Mark 5:28 AMP. See also *Strongs Exhaustive Concordance of the Bible*, entry 3004.
21. Matthew 9:22 NKJV.
22. Matthew 9:20; Luke 8:44 AMP.
23. See Numbers 15:38–41.
24. Ann Spangler and Lois Tverberg, *Sitting at the Feet of Rabbi Jesus: How the Jewishness of Jesus Can Transform Your Faith* (Grand Rapids, MI: Zondervan, 2009), 79–80.
25. See Romans 4:17.
26. See Isaiah 53:4–5; Matthew 8:16–17.
27. See 3 John 2 NKJV; Philippians 4:19.

28. As opposed to losing weight to satisfy our vanity. Daniel 1 gives an example of God honoring healthy bodies. Also see 1 Corinthians 6:19; 2 Corinthians 6:16; and 3 John 2. Although the Corinthian letters specifically apply to sexual morality, the general concept of treating one's body with the respect due it as a temple of God is a principle that applies to other healthy practices as well.
29. 1 Samuel 17:34–37.
30. 1 Samuel 17:37.
31. Matthew 12:34 NLT.
32. Philippians 4:8 MSG.
33. Ephesians 5:19 KJV.
34. Genesis 1:26 NKJV.
35. Mark 11:22–24 NKJV.
36. *Rhema Study Bible*, KJV, Red Letter Edition (Tulsa, OK: Kenneth Hagin Ministries, 1985), 69 New Testament.
37. Romans 12:3.
38. 1 Peter 5:8 AMP.
39. See Philippians 4:19 KJV.
40. John 15:7.
41. Mark 11:23 NKJV.
42. See Daniel 2:48–49.
43. See Exodus 20:3–5.
44. Daniel 3:14–15.
45. Daniel 3:16–18 NKJV.
46. Daniel 3:17 NKJV.
47. Daniel 3:18 NKJV.
48. Daniel 3:24–25 NKJV.

8: HOLDING FAST AS YOU WEATHER LIFE'S STORMS.

1. "June 22, 2003 Derecho," National Oceanic and Atmospheric Administration, http://www.spc.noaa.gov/misc/AbtDerechos/casepages/kc1982mem 2003pwrpage.htm#memphis (accessed June 10, 2009).
2. 1 Peter 5:8.
3. Jonah 1:1–12.
4. Psalm 121:2 NKJV.
5. Romans 8:31.
6. Max Lucado, *In The Grip of Grace* (Dallas, TX: Word, 1996), 174.
7. Matthew 19:29.

8. Acts 9:15.
9. Acts 27:12–13.
10. Acts 27:23–25.
11. Philippians 4:19 NKJV.
12. Mark 10:9.
13. 1 Peter 2:24.
14. Acts 27:34.
15. Acts 27:39–41.
16. See Acts 28:3.
17. Acts 28:4.
18. Acts 28:5.
19. Spangler and Tverberg, *Sitting at the Feet of the Rabbi Jesus*, 92–93. These blessings are called *berakhah* and are not unlike my experience of walking through my house, thanking God for each thing he had given me.
20. Philippians 4:8 MSG.
21. Philippians 4:8.
22. See Acts 28:6.
23. See Acts 28:7–9.
24. Robert A. Schuller, *The World's Greatest Comebacks: Eight Steps to Success* (Penguin Group, 1990).
25. Acts 28:10.
26. See Acts 28:30–31.

9: CELEBRATING THE WAYS GOD MADE YOU SPECIAL

1. Genesis 1:31.
2. Genesis 1:26 NLT.
3. Psalm 8:4–6 NLT.
4. Genesis 3:1–6.
5. Gregg Wear, *Beating the Blame Game* (Sedalia, MO: Gregg Wear, 1999), 24.
6. See Isaiah 45:18.
7. Genesis 1:26 NKJV.
8. See Matthew 7:12 MSG.
9. "George Boldt Dies; Genius of Waldorf," *New York Times,* December 6, 1916.
10. Genesis 1:10, 12, 18, 21, 25, 31 NLT.
11. The Holy Bible, New Living Translation (Wheaton, IL: Tyndale House, 1996), Genesis 1:31.
12. Dave Roever, "The Dave Roever Story," http://www.daveroever.org; de-

tails also from Dave Roever, *Scarred* (Fort Worth, TX: Roever Communications, 1995).

13. Friend, "College Football."

14. Genesis 1:31.

15. Art Linkletter, foreword to *How to Be Like Walt*, by Pat Williams with Jim Denney (Deerfield Beach, FL: Health Communications, 2004), x–xi.

16. Murray, *Michelangelo*, 195.

17. Genesis 3:10.

18. See Genesis 3:11–24.

19. Luke 7:38.

20. Luke 7:39.

21. Luke 6:35 NLT.

22. William Barclay, *New Testament Words* (Louisville, KY: Westminster John Knox, 1974), 21–22. Barclay further explores the idea of agape love as a deliberate action in the chapter "Agape and Agapan." I am indebted to the author for guiding me to this important concept.

23. Matthew 5:45.

24. Norma McCorvey with Gary Thomas, *Won by Love* (Nashville, TN: Thomas Nelson, 1997), 1–3, 51–52, 78–79, 125, 137–38, 155–60, 176, 197. Also reference Gary Thomas, "Roe v. McCorvey: What made 'Roe' betray the pro-choice cause?" *Christianity Today*, January 12, 1998. See also Norma McCorvey's Web site, http://www.leaderu.com/norma/.

25. See 1 Corinthians 13:13.

26. 1 John 4:8.

ACKNOWLEDGMENTS

1. "Have You Learned the Most Important Lesson of All?" *Parade*, May 24, 1992.

ABOUT THE AUTHOR

Motivated by his passion to see people become fearless in their convictions, limitless in their potential, and unstoppable in their God-given destiny, Frank Santora left an accounting career to become a spiritual coach and motivational speaker to thousands. His television show, *Destined to Win*, which has been aired both locally and nationally, challenges people weekly to discover the winner within themselves. A graduate of Rutgers University in New Brunswick, New Jersey, he holds a bachelor's degree in both accounting and business as well as accreditation as an ordained minister from the Rhema Bible Training Center in Broken Arrow, Oklahoma.

Pastor Santora currently serves as president of Faith Ministries and Faith Preparatory Schools, Inc., in New Milford, Connecticut, and resides in nearby Brookfield with his wife, Lisa, and their two children, Nicole and Joseph.